MY VOW
OF
SILENCE

the roughest 3 minutes of my life

TIM·STEED

MY VOW
OF
SILENCE

the roughest 3 minutes of my life

XYZZY
PRESS

Copyright © 2006 by Xyzzy Press
All rights reserved

Editorial: Tracey Bumpus
Cover and Book Design: Susan Browne
Photography: Turner Hutchison

ISBN   1-60148-000-8
ISBN-13   978-1-60148-000-2

Manufactured in the United States

This book is dedicated with a deep and unconditional love to:

my wife, Debbie, and her gentle and loving spirit,
my daughter, Meredith, and her wonderful teenage spirit!

my mother, Dot, and her enthusiastic and giving spirit,
my father, Hoyt, and his humorous story-telling spirit,

also, to my brother, Todd, and his independent and creative spirit,
to my sister, Pam, and her entertaining spirit,
to my sister, Paige, and her nurturing spirit.   .

This book is also dedicated to the memory of my brother, Vernon.
I know for a fact we will see each other again someday.
I'm thinking right after my 98th birthday works really well for me.

ACKNOWLEDGEMENTS

A special word of thanks, gratitude, and appreciation goes out to the many wonderful people who helped me take a simple dream and turn it into a simple book. Wait, that doesn't read correctly. In any event, a tip of the hat and hearty handshakes go out to:

Susan Browne—Blame her for organizing my mess of ideas and developing a fantastic book design and layout. You can also blame her for global warming.

Tracey Bumpus—Blame her for making logical, coherent sense out of my misguided tangents and ramblings. You can also blame her for having to renew your car tags every year.

Heylee Harris—Blame her for any zits, blemishes, and blackheads you might see on me at any given moment. You can also blame her when you have a root canal.

Paul Hughes—Blame him for Heylee Harris. You can also blame him for the rise in popularity of WWE SmackDown.

Turner Hutchison—Blame him for making sure the camera didn't break during the photo shoot. You can also blame him for SpongeBob SquarePants being turned into a movie.

Jason Quick—Blame him for all book imperfections, oversights, and subject matter. You can also blame him when your dog has an accident inside your house.

Ned Parks—Blame him for questionable theology and off-color material. You can also blame him when TSA agents make you take off your shoes at the airport.

Lana Shealy—Blame her for bringing me to the attention of many different people. You can also blame her for the gum on the bottom of your shoes.

Joe and Ann Stacker—Blame them for my being overweight during the front cover photo shoot as they feed me constantly. And that's about it, really. I don't want to say too much or they'll stop feeding me.

CONTENTS

INTRODUCTION

I've tried many tips, techniques, and methods over the years to find a deeper, more meaningful relationship with God. Some approaches were extremely beneficial while others were just plain brainless. For instance: I increased the minutes of my prayer time by 27 percent. I took long walks in nature. I attended church eight Sundays in a row. I was mentored online. I changed my diet to include alfalfa. I stood up and prayed in restaurants when my food arrived. I got out of bed and on my knees while it was still dark. I stopped cussing (out loud) on golf courses. I wore a dark navy suit with a solid red tie and an American flag lapel pin on Saturdays. I passed a collection plate on a city bus. I read through the Old Testament—King James Version—and actually took detailed notes that I later sold in a garage sale. And, lastly, I took a vow of silence.

Taking a vow of silence was actually pretty easy, and I felt more fulfilled and connected with God as a result. And it's still something I practice to this day. Every night from 10:30 p.m. until 6:30 a.m. I'm completely quiet. Of course it helps immensely that I'm asleep during this time period, but you do what you can to grow in your spiritual understanding.

I'm not perfect in my quest to live a pure, spiritual, and holy life; and I mess up all the time. In fact, sometimes I say things and wish I could take them back. But I can't. And it's in these moments that a true vow of silence would come in handy. Maybe you struggle with the same things I deal with, like speaking before thinking. And if a method you use in your daily routine to grow closer to God doesn't work like the many I've tried, or if you stumble with your habits and rituals in your spiritual walk just like me, don't beat yourself up over your perceived failings. Simply smile at your human limitations and ask, *What's the take-away lesson here?* Let's not let our blunders take away our joy.

And that's what this book is about—laughing at our imperfection as Christians and asking, *What have I learned?* and *How can I apply this knowledge so I can continue to grow in understanding?*

We're not a perfect people, as the world would have us be. But we worship the One who is perfect. We're not a fully loving people at all times, but we want to connect with the One who is fully Love in every moment. And we're not a continuously forgiving and merciful people, but we sing praises and offer up thanksgivings to the One who is constant in His forgiveness, His mercy, and His grace.

Enjoy the book, and remember: God loves laughter; so laugh big, laugh hard, and laugh often. And God loves servants; so serve big, serve hard, and serve often.

Prayers and love to you and yours,

Tim

chapter one

THE ROCK

"Where there is no vision,
the people perish."
—*Proverbs 29:18, KJV*

Where I live in Tennessee, the developer was blowing up the side of a mountain in a wooded area to create two new subdivisions: Deer Chase and Fox Run. And that's exactly what happened; the deer were chased off, and foxes ran for their lives. But they were making some huge boulders out of that mountain; and fancying myself a visionary of sorts, I could literally see that a giant, 14-ton boulder was just what my backyard needed. It sure didn't need any more wildlife eating out of my garden.

So I walked up to this nervous-looking man putting blasting caps on dynamite, and I asked him, "How much would you charge me to take a humongous boulder, load it in your dump truck, and then dump it in my backyard?"

And he asked, "You want to buy a rock?"

"Right," I said, "for landscaping."

He gave a quick spit, wiped his forehead with his sandwich and said, "Twenty-five bucks."

You want to talk about getting a steal of a deal? And after we agreed on the price, I told him I didn't have cash and would have to write him a check. He wasn't too happy about that, but he hopped on his diesel-powered claw machine, picked up the boulder, dropped it into the bed of his truck, and pulled up in my backyard.

He wasn't that great of a driver, as he drove all over the yard trying to get it in just the right place. And I noticed his tires were digging into the yard pretty deep, but that was OK because I really wanted that boulder.

Interesting side note to the story: My wife was at work that day. Thought you would want to know that little fun fact. It might help you understand why, at the present moment, I'm writing this story on my laptop, 400 miles away from home.

So he dumped the granite monster, narrowly missing the dog and doghouse. I gave him the check, including a tip for missing the dog; and I waited for my wife to come home. The first words out of her mouth were, "What on Earth were you thinking?"

"I wasn't thinking," I calmly stated, "I was envisioning." I will tell you unashamedly that I spent the next three weeks in traction. For a visionary, I sure didn't see that one coming. A vow of silence would have really helped me out there.

But I do love my pet rock, and he's become like a member of the family—albeit a cold, emotionless, unmoving member of the family, but a member nonetheless. I even named him Rocky Top. I think he's got a lot of cat in him because when you call him by name, he just sits and stares at you. Boulders can be so finicky.

And this whole rock episode got me thinking about our Christian walks. As children of Light, are we visionaries in Christ? If not, how can we improve to be more open to His vision? (I mean without going on a 40-day fast and actually hallucinating that your broom closet is the reincarnation of Salvador Dali...)

As children of Light, are we visionaries in Christ?

I think, first, visionaries in Christ are open to see the possibilities rather than the negativity of a situation. *What could be? What truly is God's perfect will?* Second, visionaries in Christ think of the pros and cons and the consequences for each possibility, unlike I did by not telling my wife what I was doing on my day off. Third, visionaries decide on a course of action while prayerfully developing a passion for the plan. Fourth, visionaries in Christ easily communicate that passion and vision so that others see and feel that same passion. Fifth, visionaries in Christ know the sacrifices involved and are prepared to pay whatever the price may be. And sixth, visionaries don't mind sleeping on the sofa.

Something else that might help you develop your Christian mind's eye is to study the lives of the different men in the book of Acts. That book is all about people having and understanding visions in Christ. Peter said in Acts 11:5 (KJV), "I was in the city of Joppa praying: and in a trance I saw a vision."

Let's all take that lead. Pray for what Christ's vision is for you, for America. But be careful, you might have a vision involving the purchase of a boulder. That vision, my friends, will cost you some cold, lonely nights. ☯

chapter two

ADVERTISING ON YOUR KID'S HEAD

"Finally, brothers, whatever is true,
whatever is noble, whatever is
right, whatever is pure, whatever
is lovely, whatever is admirable—if
anything is excellent or praiseworthy—
think about such things."
—*Philippians 4:8*

It's important to keep our eyes on Christ because the
world continues to create things that steal our focus. Advertising
and marketing would be big focus-stealers. From billboards to
bored Bills, advertising screams for our attention—Christians and
non-Christians alike.

An entrepreneurial dad here in Nashville—we'll call him "Bill"—
was bored with his infant son's head. More specifically, he was
bored with his infant son's medical helmet that covered his head.
It was a standard white, hospital-issue, plastic helmet with a chin

strap. *Boring.* So a friend suggested Dad put a Vanderbilt football logo sticker on the side of it.

And that thought caused Dad to have a brain far...er...storm. He decided to rent out his son's medical helmet for advertising space. And he followed through with the questionable idea and actually sold his son's helmet space on eBay for over $3,000. Now the baby goes around with "Shop Frank's Home Appliance Store" on his head.

Rent your kid's head? Come on, folks. What's next? Are you going to sponsor his stroller like they do in NASCAR?

INQUIRING STRANGER: Oh, is this your new baby?

PROUD DAD: Yes, he's 10 months.

INQUIRING STRANGER: That Dupont Paint/84 Lumber/Chick Fil-A stroller is just precious.

PROUD DAD: Let me show you his diaper!

INQUIRING STRANGER: Solid Waste Management?

PROUD DAD: I negotiated a pretty good deal on that one.

It gets worse. I stayed in a 20-story hotel out in California that had a 20-story imported beer bottle painted on the side of the building. Every day for a week I'd walk past that 20-story beer. All I could think of was, *Are they advertising to distant planets because I'm certain that aliens living on PX-56 can see it. Or maybe they're just hoping that King Kong walks past and is enticed to take a six-pack home.*

From giant beers to baby heads, advertising and marketing are attempting to steal our focus. When you see a Starbucks logo tattooed on a young lady's neck, it's time to focus not on the absurdity of life but on the mercy and love of the cross. Well, don't completely ignore the absurdity of life because there are plenty of big laughs to be had there. ☺

MUST-HEAR SERMON:

'I've Got Ants in My Pants' and Other Funny Sayings of John the Baptist

chapter three

IF YOU CAN SEE IT, THEN WHY'D YOU STEP IN IT?

"But small is the gate and narrow
the road that leads to life,
and only a few find it."
—*Matthew 7:14*

My Christian walk is like a hike through a Middle Tennessee cow pasture. It's delightful—but dangerous. And on my walk, I marvel at God's greatness and majesty all the time; but I still step in way too many of life's cow patties. And then I end up spending a lot of time cleaning off the soles of my shoes, and that's not good. When I could be serving, I'm stopping to clean.

For me, the cow patties in my Christian walk represent the habits and rituals that keep me from a deeper, more meaningful walk with Jesus, who, by the way, went through life on Earth without stepping in a single patty. Now according to Scripture, His disciples stepped in a few; and I'm thinking that could be one of the reasons He washed their feet. Or not.

Now some cow patties I'm very familiar with, and I know where they are in the pasture because at one point in life I've stepped in them. These are actually called *cow chips* now because they've dried out. But I don't step on the cow chips, nor do I pick them up and fling them across the field like a bovine-processed Whammo Frisbee. I just keep my head up and my feet walking.

My earthly goal is to make it though the cow pasture and, by God's mercy, end up at the narrow gate that takes me to a much bigger and better pasture. On my bad days I think that gate might not even be there at all. But I keep going back to the ancient letters that were written by some people who made it through and around the cow patties before me. And these people actually wore sandals on their feet, so I guess they know what they're talking about because they had a lot at stake during their hike.

One of the ancient letters stated that Jesus said the gate is there, but it's narrow and few people actually find it. Sometimes on my walk I think I see it; but then, without warning…SQUISH! Hello, fresh patty. When that happens, I take my eyes off the gate and put it on the mess that has to be cleaned.

One of the major problems of my Christian walk is forgetting about the hidden cow patties. Like on days when the pasture grass is really green and soft, and it's so wonderfully comfortable that I decide to take off my shoes and walk barefoot. And then, SQUISH! It's up between the toes. By the way, my wife says I have ugly toes; but that's for a different book altogether, like a pop-up book or coffee table book.

I think materialism would be a cow patty for me. It seems that sometimes when my prayer life is good, my meditation times are productive and centering, my Bible study is producing enlightenment, and I'm serving others in love, I'll go out and buy something electronic and step right in a patty the size of a VW Beetle.

If I can see the cross that sits on top of the narrow gate that teaches and instructs me, then why do I keep stepping in cow patties?

One recent example was when I went out and starting looking at portable DVD players. *I need it for my many plane rides,* I told myself. *It helps block out the noise from crying babies.* That's a major cow patty *a la mode. Wait, I also need a professional digital video camera with wireless mic to tape my speeches and shows. And it sure would be nice if I had a digital still camera that could download right to my e-mail…but, what if I had that giant, flat-screen TV for SEC football action on Saturdays? And wouldn't life be so much better if I had a vintage Gibson Les Paul electric guitar?* The answer to that last question would be a resounding, heartfelt "yes." See? I can just smell that cow patty I'm getting ready to step in.

I always wonder, *If I can see the cross that sits on top of the narrow gate that teaches and instructs me, then why do I keep stepping in cow patties?* I focus on Jesus, but that old habit or ritual is suddenly deposited right in front of me to navigate. Sometimes I think all my stepping in cow patties might help with character building in the long run. Sometimes I think it helps so I can tell others in the pasture where cow patties might be located.

In our hike though the pasture of life, let's clean our feet as quickly as we can and as often as we can so we can keep our focus on the narrow gate. And don't forget to go cow tipping every chance you get. The more cows on their backs, the less cow patties we have to navigate. And in my life, that would be helpful. That and a vintage 1960 sunburst Gibson Les Paul.

We'll talk about the amp later. ◉

chapter four

BBQ RESTAURANTS

"Horrifying Vegetarians Since 1995."
—*Sign spotted at Boss Hawg's BBQ*
& Catering, Topeka, Kansas

I like restaurants to have a giant, fiberglass replica

or cartoon picture outside of the actual animal that's being served.
I just want to drive down the road in my car, look at the exterior of
the restaurant, and know without a doubt what they do best.

> **WIFE:** I don't care where we eat, just pick a place.
> **ASTUTE HUSBAND:** What about that rotating pig head? See
> it up on the roof over there?
> **WIFE:** Think it's any good?
> **ASTUTE HUSBAND:** He's wearing a chef's hat. What's that
> tell you?

The thing that somewhat bothers me about putting up a cartoon
picture or fiberglass reproduction of the main entrée is that these
animals look to be generally happy. And the reason they're happy,

I've figured out, is that they're the ones holding the cooking utensils.

You've seen them: the catfish with a skillet in his fin, frying up a mess o' young. You've got a bull with a ring in his nose holding a steak knife and wearing a bib. In Texas, I saw a 10-foot statue of a chicken dropping napalm out of a helicopter. No wonder they're smiling; they're animal cannibals. But I say as long as they don't eat me, I don't really care who kills what. Just get me whatever I'm eating in 20 minutes or less.

Tim's Taxidermy Rule: The more animals you see shot, stuffed, and mounted on the wall, the better the food.

Now once you walk inside one of these places, Tim's Taxidermy Rule goes into effect. And that rule simply states: The more animals you see shot, stuffed, and mounted on the wall, the better the food. You see seven deer, four ducks, and a raccoon wearing sunglasses—you've just entered this side of Heaven. In fact, if they have a full-sized stuffed bear, elk, or moose over in the corner, my recommendation is you take home one of their homemade pies. And then you will be in Heaven—from over-eating.

Of course, Tim's Taxidermy Rule only applies to BBQ joints and steak houses. It doesn't work at, let's say, Italian, Mexican, or some Asian restaurants.

Now, does what I'm writing on BBQ restaurants have any spiritual significance or biblical teaching points to help us live a more brilliant Christ-centered life? No, sadly it doesn't. I just wondered if you've noticed what I've noticed when I've eaten at one of these places.

You can go on to the next essay now while I contemplate if the vow of silence should be applied to the written word, as well. ☯

chapter five

CELL-PHONE COMMUNICATION

"Steve Fawcett has crashed his
balloon while attempting to
take it around the world.
... You know why he crashed?
He was talking on his cell phone."
—*Jay Leno*

One thing I like about cell phones is cell-phone etiquette.
You can actually tell people while on the phone with them that you
"don't have many minutes left," and that quickly brings the conversation to a close.

I hear people use excuses like:

"Hey, I'm running out of minutes..."

"Look, I can't waste my minutes on this right now..."

"I can't afford my minutes to be eaten up on this..."

So by using my unique talent of eavesdropping on thousands of
public conversations in airports across America, I can tell that the

people on the other end are always fine with this. No problems, no hurt feelings. They understand.

I've also taken note that if the minutes excuse doesn't work, you can also tell them you don't have a strong signal; and that wraps things up as well.

"Ralph, I've only got one bar…"

"Got a half-a-bar, can't talk…"

"My bars are gone…hello?"

And once again, people are fine with this. Everyone accepts this, and no one really gets upset with a lack of minutes or receding bars.

Enter creative thinking. Or as I like to say, "I'm about to get myself in trouble."

To gain more control of my time, I decided to use this theory of cell-phone etiquette with my face-to-face conversations. If it works over the phone, why wouldn't it work in person? The answer is: it does. Let's say you pass your boss in the hallway:

PSYCHOSOMATIC BOSS: I'm obsessing about the status of the McClunky account. What's the latest that I didn't know three minutes ago?

SHINING, SUBORDINATE YOU: I'm sorry, I'm out of minutes. See me next month.

Or, if someone drones on and on in a meeting and catches you daydreaming:

MEETING-MANIPULATOR COWORKER: Could you wake up, please? Are you with us?

AWESOME, SHOULD-BE-EMPLOYEE-OF-THE-MONTH YOU: I don't have any bars for this meeting. Hold on let me check; yep, no bars.

Don't be afraid to use this system, as it works like a Wednesday-night church volunteer kitchen worker. And the best part is, people really don't get upset because everyone is familiar with how cell phone etiquette works. In fact, my plan works so well, I've assigned minutes to everything and everybody in my life. I started with my preacher. (Got your attention, didn't I?)

Once you control your time, then
you control your life; and once you
control your life, you can begin to
really focus on the things that matter.

UP-FOR-SAINTHOOD ME: Hey, Pastor Mike, check this out. I've assigned you 100 minutes from the pulpit per month. That's 25 minutes per Sunday. You think you can get your point across in 25 minutes?

CEASELESS-SERMON MIKE: Sure I can Tim, but what about when there's a fifth Sunday in the month?

UP-FOR-SAINTHOOD ME: I sleep in. I'm out of minutes, remember?

CEASELESS-SERMON MIKE: I'll pray hard for you, son.

UP-FOR-SAINTHOOD ME: You better fast for me too 'cause a gossipy deacon told me your cholesterol level is way out of whack.

Yet another time I should have taken on a vow of silence. And amazingly, I've not been nominated for a single church committee, nor have I been assigned any type of church leadership position. (That, as you've guessed by now, is a huge positive in itself.) So look around and assign minutes and/or bars to everything you can; and, before you know it, you'll be more in control of your time. And once you control your time, then you control your life; and once you control your life, you can begin to really focus on the things that matter—things like serving God with your talents, abilities, and financial resources. Oh, keep in mind this minutes-and-bars-thing is only a theory. I have yet to actually apply any of these brilliant concepts during my fleeting and sporadic moments of reality. ☺

chapter six

PASSION OR FASHION?

"Many come to bring their clothes
to church rather than themselves."
—*Thomas Fuller*

Here's what I want you to do. I want you to get something to write with and to write on. Go ahead. Get up and go get it. I'll be waiting. Really, I'm serious. Get something to write with if you don't have anything handy.

You're still sitting there, aren't you? That's OK. But if you did get something to write with and on, congratulations: You win a hearty "thank you" and a three-year subscription to *Cat Fancy En Espanol*. Look for it in the mail soon.

Now, I'd like to do a little word association with you so hence the pen and paper to help capture your thoughts. You ready? Great.

Write down everything you can think of when you see this phrase: *Church clothes*. Go. Write and don't stop to edit yourself. I'll brainstorm as well.

Church clothes:

- stuffy

- restricting

- fancy

- tight collar

- stiff and starchy

- uncomfortable

- nice

- clean

- smell good

- fake ties

- short-term

- bright on Easter

- white shoes/Pat Boone

- can be hung back up on the hanger when you get home

- can be worn again at church in three weeks because no one really remembers what you wear to church

- too much fuss

How'd you do? Any similarities between my list and yours? Did you completely blow off the exercise and just read my list? That's OK; I would have done the same thing because when I read a book I just want to be entertained. I really don't want to write down any type of a list or add anything up or find some kind of mathematical pattern.

However, I have another question for you. Do you think it matters what you wear to church? Are jeans OK on a Sunday?

What about shorts during the summer for Sunday morning worship? Is a tie needed for a Wednesday night vespers service? There are many different answers to these questions depending on who you ask and where you worship.

So now that I've warmed you up a bit. Here's the ultimate question: Does God care what we are wearing when we worship Him at church? Keep in mind, we can and should worship God anywhere and at any time. But for now, we're just talking about at church.

Does God care what we are wearing when we worship Him at church?

To help us answer that question, let's see what God told Samuel in 1 Samuel 16:7, which reads, "Man looks at the outward appearance, but the Lord looks at the heart." OK, so we've found the answer. Now I'm guessing that in most cases your parents might care what you dress like for church, your spouse might care what you dress like ("You're not wearing *that* are you?"), the church might care what you dress like, certain religions might care what you dress like, and your friends will for sure let you know when you missed the mark with your outfit. But God cares most about how your heart is dressed. That's what He told Samuel.

On the other hand, does that give you the freedom to wear a loin cloth and combat boots to church if your heart is pure? Well, the revolutionary Tarzan look might be a distraction to others in a corporate worship setting, so you may want to consider wearing—at the very least—a T-shirt, shorts, and Crocs. But God cares about our compassion. He cares about our love. He cares about our mercy. He cares about our passion for serving and worshiping Him. If we take care of those things, what to put on our bodies will take care of itself.

So to help me set my attitude for the day, some of the questions I ask myself in the morning are, *What am I going to put on my heart today? How will I dress it up? Will I dress it up to be clean and neat and wrinkle free? Will I have a forgiving heart today, or will I blow my car horn at the guy who cuts me off in rush-hour traffic?* I want to walk out of my house and have people compliment me not on my clothes but on my heart.

"Wow, great-looking heart you have there, Tim."

"Oh, this old thing? It's just something I threw on at the last minute."

It's all about heart. The next time you walk out of your house remember 1 Samuel 16:7 and ask yourself, *Does my heart show through my clothes?* If not, then ask yourself what you need to do to make that happen. And then simply go out and dress it up to the nines. ❡

chapter seven

BEING LATE FOR SUNDAY SCHOOL

"A Sunday School is a prison in
which children do penance for the
evil conscience of their parents."
—*H.L. Mencken*

There are some Sundays when I miss Sunday School

for the heck of it. Procrastination, I guess. I'll miss Sunday School
and then go to church. Or, sometimes I miss both. In the world of
go, go, go, go, Sunday—as well as Saturday—is a good day to rest.
God rested on Sunday, so it should be good enough for me, right?

It's also very easy to find an excuse to miss Sunday School when
you attend a megachurch. You can say, "Traffic's too bad. … I get
road rage in the parking lot. … Everybody will be there. … I can't
find a seat in the bathroom. …" or many other excuses.

So I really don't feel bad or guilty or sad that I miss Sunday
School on occasion. In fact, I'm writing this right now on a Sunday
morning at 9:15. Sunday School starts in 15 minutes, and I'm still in

my sleepwear (read: old T-shirt and boxer shorts). Now, I *am* going to church today, OK? Just not Sunday School.

Sometimes when I'm torn in my decision to stay home or go to Sunday School, I'll write out a pro/con list of why to stay home.

Cons for staying home:

- Will miss doughnuts and thick, black coffee.
- Will miss small talk while eating doughnuts and drinking thick, black coffee.
- Will miss lesson prepared by expert teacher.
- Will miss opportunity to throw out sarcastic remark during lesson at said expert teacher, possibly generating big laugh at his expense. (This is the one I really struggle with.)

Pros for staying home:

- Don't have to comb my hair for awhile.
- Can prepare/drink my own coffee made to my specifications.
- Don't have to shave right away.
- Can see what cartoons are on.
- Can play the guitar quietly. (My wife's still in bed; and that, my friends, is for a whole different book.)
- Can get creative by experimenting with a new grits dish for breakfast.
- Can walk around in sleepwear and scratch at my leisure.
- Don't have to put on restricting "church clothes" until last minute.
- Can take a shower when it's convenient for me.

(Notice how a lot of these deal with personal hygiene? That's sad—pray for me.)

So as you can plainly see, the pros for staying home and going only to church far outweigh the cons. And the only time the list leans to the favor of the cons is when Ed and Estelle Smoot bring in their famous sausage and kudzu wraps. And they only do that once a year, but that's a Sunday School class your arteries can't afford to miss. ☺

MUST-HEAR SERMON:

If Sitting on the Back Pew in Church Were Dirt, I'd Be 14 Acres

chapter eight

LOUIS BOYD

"As iron sharpens iron, so one
man sharpens another."
—*Proverbs 27:17*

Louis Boyd is a great Christian man.

Let me rephrase that. My friend, Louis Boyd, associate pastor
of Florida Boulevard Baptist Church in Baton Rouge, Louisiana, is
battling cancer. He's suffering from a steadily progressing disease
in the love and light of Christ, and he's giving all the glory to God.

That's only one of the many reasons that Louis Boyd is a great
Christian man. I know he's a wonderful husband and a very cool
dad. I've seen him many, many times interact with his family in all
types of situations. I know he's a friend to everyone, from seniors
to bed babies, to Christians and non-Christians alike. I know he
has an outstanding sense of humor. He's one of those guys who
makes you smile as soon as you see him because you know laughs
will quickly follow. And I also know that as Louis is moving closer to
Heaven, he's still leading people to Jesus in a personal way.

I first met Louis when I was a member of Downtown Baptist Church in Orlando, Florida. He was on staff there, but what I remember most about him was his creativity and humor. He made the announcements during the worship service, and all you had to do to start smiling was watch him get up from the pew and start moving that lanky frame of his toward the platform. I would look around at the congregation, and everyone would be smiling because they knew in just a few moments they would be laughing.

But Louis wasn't just entertaining us during the announcements. He was using his God-given gift of creativity to encourage us. And I really loved that about him. He would present his messages in the most imaginative and unusual ways. He would use props such as a megaphone or a cardboard box or a hat, and we would laugh and smile as he gave his presentation. I always loved it when he would fill in for our pastor, Dr. Bill Montgomery, and preach a sermon. Louis was serious about God's love, but he presented the message in such an engaging way that even the short-attention-span kids would stop squirming and listen.

He once said during a Wednesday night service that if Jesus were just an enlightened spiritual teacher—like a lot of people in the world claim Him to be—then you would have to also admit that Jesus was a certified lunatic. The reason being is that Jesus claimed to be the Son of God. Jesus also claimed to be the *only* way to God. No sane, intelligent, enlightened teacher instructing people in the ways of love and forgiveness would claim that He was the only way to God, would He? So Louis said you had a choice: to believe Jesus was—and is—who He claimed to be, or to believe Jesus was really cuckoo insane.

Louis wasn't just entertaining us during the announcements. He was using his God-given gift of creativity to encourage us.

The last time I saw Louis was just about a month ago after I had given a seminar in Louisiana. I was waiting for him outside of the hotel; and he drove up, got out of his car, and I started smiling because I knew in just a few moments I would be laughing. I told him he actually looked pretty good, and he flashed that sparkling grin and said, "It's all smoke and mirrors." I laughed, and it felt really good.

But I knew we couldn't talk long as I was in a time crunch. I had a flight back to Nashville in about an hour-and-a-half, so we decided just to visit there in the hotel lobby. He told me outrageous stories, and I laughed. He told me how God was blessing him during the sickness, and I was awed. He told me how the Holy Spirit used him to lead a young lady dying of cancer to give her life to Christ, and I was inspired. And he told me about his wife and son, and my heart began to ache.

At one point during our seamless conversation, I realized that if I didn't get up and leave right at that very moment, I would miss the last flight out of Baton Rouge to Nashville. I would miss sleeping in my bed, and I would miss being with my family. And then I looked at Louis as he was deep into another story. So I took on a vow of silence and decided to not tell him that I was going to miss my flight just to spend time with him. Instead, I sunk back deeper into my chair, unhurriedly re-crossed my legs, and laughed a warm, wonderful laugh; a laugh that was compliments of Mr. Louis Boyd.

Sometimes we have to remember that it's not about us and making *our* meetings and answering *our* phones and catching *our* flights. It's about sacrificing these small moments of life when they come to us and giving others what they might need. In Louis' case—his body worn out and ravaged from the fight against the deadly cancer—he simply needed an audience. And for someone who can so easily make people smile and laugh, an audience was an honor for me to provide.

chapter nine

BLACK HOLE FOR BIBLES

"People really need to spend
time in the Bible getting to know
the God they claim to love."
—*Willie Aames*

At my super-megachurch, Brentwood Baptist, we have a
"Lost and Found" table. You'll find everything on that table from
purses to people, but what they really have the most of is Bibles.
I've actually made it a ritual to walk by the table on Wednesday
nights and count them. I don't have much of a life, and what little
life I do have is apparently self-righteous. But that's for a different
therapy session all together.

Last night I counted an amazing 22 Bibles on the "Lost and
Found" table. What's even more amazing is that most of these
Bibles have been on the table for months. And some of these
Bibles even have the owners' names printed on the front! These
are the ones I wonder about. You figure if someone went to the
trouble to emboss his name on a genuine, leather-bound, No. 7
dye, red-letter, gold-flake page edging, steamed rice paper,

easy-eye print with four ribbon markers KJV Bible, he'd care enough to track it down.

I wonder how you lose your Bible at church and then not do an exhaustive search to get it back. Actually the only thing that would be exhaustive about the search would be getting up out of your favorite chair and going down to the church to pick it up.

But think about it: You lose your car keys and your household comes to a screeching halt. You're running around in a panic, screaming, "Has anybody seen my keys? Tammy, look under the sofa! Max, check the toilet! No, I don't care if you leave the seat up, just hurry!"

But we lose our Bible at church, and we simply don't care. My theory is we don't care because we don't remember that we lost it in the first place. How can you care about something you don't remember? I think the reason we don't remember we lost it in the first place is because we don't use it every day like we do our car keys. (Note to self: Tim, make sure your Bible is as important as your car keys, wallet, TV remote, playing blues guitar, and following Tennessee football.)

Our "Lost and Found" table is kind of a depressing place, actually. All you have to do is look at one of these Bibles and realize that each one has a tragic story to tell. One had duct tape all over it to help with the binding. It must really be special for someone to try to extend the life with duct tape. But now the forgotten NADTS (New American Duct Tape Standard) is used only to collect dust. Unloved and alone, it sits unread. They shouldn't call it "Lost and Found"; they should call it the "Black Hole for Bibles."

Now I know this might take some advanced planning, but if you do tend to use your Bible as a prop on Sundays, and you don't plan on finding it if you do lose it, then lose the thing where it

---

I think the reason we don't
remember we lost it in the first
place is because we don't use it
every day like we do our car keys.

---

might just make a difference. Lose it on the metro train or in an airport. Lose it at a theme park or at the beach. Lose it in a college football stadium that holds 107,000 people. Lose it where someone might just pick it up and read it, understand it, and then apply the teachings in a positive and uplifting manner.

In fact, if you're reading this right now and wondering, "Come to think of it, I haven't seen my Bible lately," then get out of your favorite chair and go directly to your church and reclaim your lost Bible. Then immediately take it and re-lose it in a place where it has a chance to have a lasting impact. Or, you can do like I did and simply attach it to your key ring.

The choice is yours. ☯

chapter ten

BOMB-THREAT BLUES

"Don't you know that you
yourselves are God's temple and
that God's Spirit lives in you?"
—*1 Corinthians 3:16*

I was in the process of boarding a Southwest plane at
LAX when various official types plus a skinny, under-fed dog went
rushing past us with panic on their faces. Seems they found a note
protruding from a *Sky Mall* magazine saying there was a bomb
on the plane. I would guess someone objected to the price of
the solar-powered garden rake with the digital foreign language
course attachment. And suddenly faced with escalating worthless
gadget prices, this clueless person wrote a threatening note on a
drink napkin.

The thing that gets me about the bomb threat is that I developed
a very negative attitude in just a matter of moments. And I wasn't
upset that someone could have been trying to kill me and everyone on board; my attitude went sour because the bomb threat
delayed my flight, and I was going to be extremely late to my final

destination. I was inconvenienced for two hours, and I let that interpretation of events turn me into a complainer/whiner/baby.

But I had a plan to turn my attitude around. I immediately launched into various religious practices to regain my composure. I recited a standardized prayer I learned in the third grade, but that didn't work because I kept thinking of how third grade almost traumatized me for life. I wanted to sing a classic hymn out loud, but I couldn't find a 200-year-old pipe organ to accompany me; so that didn't work.

> When the outside world burdens
> us with confusion and stress, the
> inside spiritual world provides
> a yoke of rest for our souls.

Actually, the only other religious thing I could think of that might even remotely work was to take an offertory. And you can guess how that one would have gone over. Man, being religious on the spur of the moment is difficult to do, especially when you're stressed out. So I just sat and stewed until they brought us another airplane.

However, now that I look back, I should have been focusing on getting in touch with the Spirit that lives within me. Instead, I jumped right into looking for relief-by-the-religious-numbers, so to speak. I thought I needed something like, "Seven Easy Steps to Being Religious Right Now." But what I really needed at that moment was to visit with a personal friend named Jesus. But I kind of forgot about Him because I was thinking about me. *Holy Spirit, who?*

And this is where I always want to kick myself. Why don't I get it? When I seem to struggle the most is when I let the outside world interfere with my inside world. And it's always my choice. I can either interpret events as: "I'm not getting what I want," or I can interpret events—like a bogus bomb threat—as a simple opportunity to sit and take on the yoke of Christ. Sometimes I really wish I could take on a vow of silence when it comes to my negative thoughts. And maybe I can.

In Matthew 11:29 Jesus teaches us, "Take my yoke upon you and learn from me, for I am gentle and humble in heart, and you will find rest for your souls."

When the outside world burdens us with confusion and stress, the inside spiritual world provides a yoke of rest for our souls. I need to remember that. I think I'll put Matthew 11:29 on a sticky note and slap it on my forehead for a week—or longer. Now that would be the bomb. ☉

chapter eleven

CRACKER BARREL

*"I went to a restaurant that serves
'breakfast at any time.' So I ordered
French toast during the Renaissance."*
—Steven Wright

I don't enjoy restaurants that put random stuff on their walls. Cracker Barrel would be a prime example. To me, it's like corporate headquarters said, "To save decorating costs, let's raid a junk yard."

I went there this afternoon, and it all came back to me why I don't enjoy eating there. On the wall next to my booth there was a wash tub, a bent fly swatter, and a set of box springs. It's like having lunch in a landfill. If the FBI truly wants to find Jimmy Hoffa, they'll search a Cracker Barrel.

I also don't like them hanging up those old black-and-white photos of unhappy people who were last alive during the Great Depression. And these stiffs aren't smiling. They're watching you eat pancakes. That's not very thoughtful for the patrons who are battling paranoid schizophrenia.

They also put up rusty advertising signs of companies that have been out of business for years: "Texas Tooth Powder—Brush your tooth today." I'm sorry, but thinking about someone's lack of dental care is not at all appetizing. It is, without a doubt, a very depressing restaurant. If you think about it, you're actually surrounded by garbage, death, and failure. Instead of bringing you mints with your bill, your server should fill prescriptions, "Here's the check and the after-dinner meds. Hope you feel better soon."

Now I might be going to the extremes, but it is true that surrounding yourself with a certain environment will make you emotionally feel a certain way, if you let it. If your relationship with Christ seems a little stale, and your prayers don't seem to be doing any good, look for ways to continue to surround yourself and cover yourself with Christ in as many creative ways as possible. Lamentations 3:44 teaches, "You have covered yourself with a cloud so that no prayer can get through."

If you feel out of synch in your spiritual walk, then consider covering yourself like a Cracker Barrel wall. But just don't surround yourself with all types of junk like they do. Surround and cover yourself with Christ. ☉

MUST-HEAR SERMON:

If You Can't Take the Heat, Don't Visit My Parents' Home— They Keep It Like an Oven in There

chapter twelve

BE STILL?
YOU'VE GOT TO BE KIDDING.

"Ask me about my vow of silence."
—*Button seen on a Tibetan monk*

Long-dead Italian economist Paredo developed something
called the 80-20 rule. Such as in business, 80 percent of your results
come from 20 percent of your work. Or in the church world, 80
percent of the budget is provided by 20 percent of the members.
I've even noticed at a church picnic, 80 percent of the food is
eaten by 20 percent of the people. I know; I'm the captain of that
20 percent. By the way, I'd like to publicly thank anyone who has
ever brought a homemade cobbler to one of these functions.

Now since this 80-20 rule is some type of universal law, I decided
to apply this principle to my prayer life. I spend 20 percent of my
prayer time talking to God, while I spend the other 80 percent
listening. Sounds great, right? Well, it does sound great. However,
it's a tough thing to actually master.

As you can guess, it's no problem for me to ask the Holy Spirit
for something. In fact, I excel at this, "God, grant me this or that;

and help this person and that person with their health problems; and how about world peace before my next dental appointment rolls around? Oh, and I need a good parking spot near the front of the store. In Jesus' name...amen."

But then when it comes to listening, I don't have time because life is happening all around me. And if I do happen to have time to listen, then getting control of my mind so it doesn't wander off in multiple directions is almost an impossible task.

So I'm working on taking a vow of silence with my brain. I've found out that to properly silence my brain, I cannot rush the process. I need to know up front that I will have an extended period of uninterrupted time in which I'm surrounded by total, deep-space nothingness. No phones, kids, dog, TV, Internet, newspaper, or combat Twister during this time.

I have a couple plans of attack to carry out my mission. One thing I do is to imagine an empty cross. If I'm in the process of coming to the state of quietness and I start thinking about what's in the refrigerator, I'll picture a cross and hold it there for as long as I can. In a few seconds, I'm no longer focusing on the hickory-smoked, medium-rare, deli-sliced roast beef (hold the mayo).

Another way I quiet myself is by both seeing and thinking about a certain word. I'll pick a fruit of the Spirit, and I'll both see and think about that word. Sometimes I'll repeat it out loud as well, "Joy. Joy. Almond. Joy. Need ... Almond ... Joy." Be careful about the words you pick to focus on. And don't pray when your body is craving sugar.

Another way to still my continually rambling thoughts is to focus on breathing from the diaphragm. I've learned that once I focus on my breathing, then my mind slows down to having no thoughts at all. Sadly, my wife accuses me of diaphragmatic breathing constantly: "What were you thinking when you mixed towels, whites, darks, delicates, and the cat into the washing machine? Oh, you weren't thinking. You were breathing from your diaphragm."

It's in the clearing of the mind that we come to sort out life's complex issues: "Should I have ice cream for dinner or just tater tots?"

However, I believe it's in the listening to God that you'll see changes in your life. It's in the listening that we find a peace and contentment that the apostle Paul wrote about in many of his letters. It's in the listening that we find instruction and guidance. It's in the listening that we experience a deep and pure love. It's in the clearing of the mind that we come to sort out life's complex issues: "Should I have ice cream for dinner or just tater tots?"

A really cool psalm you may have read is, "Be still and know that I am God." Now where the verse is located in the Book of Psalms is not really important right now. You can search for it later, and I encourage you to do so. But what is important right now is that as you read this, make a commitment to being still for an extended period once a day. Still the body; still the mind; still the anxiety; and in doing so, you might just gain a deep and lasting spiritual solution to a problem you've been praying about.

You may ask, "God, is my purpose to enjoy a double stack of pecan pancakes or to teach ESL to the members of my community?"

And if you still your mind, the answer is clear. Just make sure you heat the maple syrup first. ☺

chapter thirteen

DONATING BLOOD

"The Red Cross in its nature, its aims
and purposes, and consequently,
its methods, is unlike any other
organization in the country."
—*Clara Barton*

I recommend giving blood to the Red Cross; preferably, you'll want to donate someone else's. However, if you can't arrange that, then donate your own blood. Not only do you help your fellow man, you learn to increase your threshold to pain. Both build character.

As a rather infrequent donor at the Red Cross, I was loaded up with paperwork, filling out all kinds of probing questions about my personal history like, "Have you ever watched a prison movie set in 1980's Africa with a liberal Freudian psychoanalyst?" I left that one blank because I really wasn't sure of the time period of the movie.

Then, after completing the unique questionnaire, I presented my papers to the dust-covered-but-still-breathing lady at the general information desk.

"Will they see me soon?" I asked her.

"Have a seat, frisky," she mumbled.

So I waited. And as I waited, I watched all the volunteers and employees in the lobby. One of these employees was the security guard named Elmer. Something I noticed was that Elmer was *armed*. Why would the Red Cross have an armed security guard named Elmer? Is the Red Cross a terrorist target? I surely don't think bandits or desperados would hit it, unless they were part of some satanic group that was in need of three cases of O positive for a freakish ritual involving a bucket and a prom queen.

Something else I noticed while waiting and watching in the lobby. There seems to be a pecking order of who gets to go back and give blood quickly and who doesn't. And just because I was in the "who-doesn't-give-quickly" line doesn't mean these next few sentences are sour grapes. OK, fine, they are.

But, man, frequent donors receive the royal treatment from the Red Cross. People smile at them and call them by their first names. Frequent donors get the fully electric, leather lounger with seven adjustable positions and heated fanny pad; I got a plastic beach chair with a broken cup holder. The frequent donors watched a digital, flat-screen TV with DVD; I got a cracked Etch-a-Sketch with a missing knob.

The frequent donors are also members of something called the "Preferred Pints Points Program"—or the "4-P Club" as they like to refer to it. They earn valuable prizes like vacations and free air fares. The only thing I earned was having the circulation in my arm cut off by a cotton ball taped and wrapped too tightly to my arm.

So I learned a painful lesson. If you do decide to give blood, it's better to give frequently.

The same is true of our spiritual lives, isn't it? It's hard to feel liked a plugged-in member at church if I just show up randomly. Sometimes when I miss a couple of Sundays in a row I feel out of synch with the relationships I have with other believers. I have a harder time getting into the flow of worship and praising God during the service. (And worst of all, I miss out on all the free doughnuts and coffee.)

Maybe if I make a solid commitment to becoming a frequent attender at church, I would perhaps feel more of a sense of belonging.

Maybe—just maybe—if I make a solid commitment to becoming a frequent donor …er… attender at church, I would perhaps feel more of a sense of belonging. And I bet I would receive some of the perks the regulars seem to get. Things like that heated, extra-plush reclining pew with an up-to-the-minute news and sports ticker. Of course, the only bad thing about the cushy seats is that they're on the very front row in the sanctuary. But, just like giving blood at the Red Cross, sitting on the front row in church builds character. ☺

chapter fourteen

BATTLE OF THE BIRDFEEDER

"You can't be friends with a squirrel!
A squirrel is just a rat with a cuter outfit."
—*Sarah Jessica Parker*

I am in a battle to the death with a gang of squirrels. That's right; I've declared war on the hoodlum, no-good gang of bushy-tailed thieves. They're birdfeeder thugs, actually; and I'm here to take back the birdfeeder for the poor, defenseless birds. And I'm losing, but I'm never going to give up. To all squirrels I say: I will be persistent.

However, it's such an uphill battle. For instance, I went outside to enjoy my Bible study and quiet time this morning; and there were 10 malicious, tattoo-covered squirrels feasting all around and on the birdfeeder. You can't enjoy time with God when those Nutkin punks are eating on sunflower seeds that aren't theirs. So I chased them off by waving my arms in a highly erratic circular motion and making a bizarre grunting sound. My neighbors seem to get a kick out of watching me act in this peculiar fashion, as they'll gather all the family members on their back patio.

Of course, when I act weird, the squirrels run up the trees and wait for me to go inside. Then when I go back inside, that's when they'll perform another squirrel sortie on the birdfeeder. Now I have tried all types of strategies in my battle of the birdfeeder. First thing I did was to purchase a squirrel-proof birdfeeder. The second thing I did was to learn there is no such thing as a squirrel-proof birdfeeder. They'll jump on it, eat through it, and hang upside on the bird perch while munching on the stolen seed. They're mocking me, and they're proud of it.

I collected a pile of small rocks and put them by my back door to throw at the birdfeeder. I don't actually throw at the squirrels, but I hope to hit the birdfeeder and make a loud enough noise to scare them off. I think they figured out that plan; so they just sit and wait till I'm out of ammo, and then they go back to their embezzled buffet.

So as a last resort I bought a super soaker. I would spray them, but I don't think it was really effective as most started showing up with beach toys. But then a "friend" showed me how to make a flame thrower out of the super soaker. Folks, don't try this at home; but it really works. And if you don't mind burning down your trees, it's very effective. No trees equals no squirrels. It also equals no birds, but sometimes you have to sacrifice something.

I will tell you this: I'm never going to give up in my battle with the tree-hugging rodents. I may be losing, but I press on and forge ahead in my quest to rid my birdfeeder of all squirrels. Paul's words remind us in Romans 2:7, "To those who by *persistence* in doing good seek glory, honor and immortality, he will give eternal life" (italics mine). As you can see, this Scripture has nothing to with fighting squirrels. It's about persistence. And I do seek glory, honor, and immortality in my neighborhood as "the man who never wavered and eventually defeated the squirrels." I want people to point to me and say, "He's the one. He did it. Let's honor him with a backyard BBQ pool party."

So what personal battles are you facing at the moment? What tactics have you tried, and why weren't they successful? Maybe the one missing ingredient in your quest for victory is persistence.

So you fail. So what? So you struggle. Isn't that part of living life?

Modify your strategies and approaches to your battles and then be persistent. I really do believe persistence prevails when doing battle. That is, unless the battle involves raising a couple of teenagers. And if that's the case, the only things you can do are pray and stay out of the way. ☺

MUST-HEAR SERMON:

I Never Promised You a Rose Garden, But I Can Set You Up with Some Kudzu

chapter fifteen

GOD'S GRITS

"In Tennessee and at Waffle House, grits are 'king.'"
—www.grits.com

It is my belief that grits are the perfect food. Sorry God—and no offense—but grits are way better than manna. You ever hear of anyone adding smoked cheddar cheese with a small chunk of fatback to manna?

Now my Mammaw made wonderful grits. Her formula was grits + sausage grease + sugar + real butter = outrageously high cholesterol followed by an early death. She was a great cook and the local mortician's best friend.

Anyway, back to the questionable premise that grits are the perfect food. Now before you say, "God made manna, so that would be the perfect food!" Let me just say that God made corn and a steamroller, so He's responsible for grits as well. However, here's the main difference between manna and grits: If God had instead rained down grits from Heaven, the Israelites would have made it to the Promised Land a lot faster.

HUNGRY JEWISH WALKER #1: Grits! Our prayers are answered!

HUNGRY JEWISH WALKER #237: They taste great, and my stamina has increased tenfold!

HUNGRY JEWISH WALKER #1: Yes, we should be able to cover 40 years of desert wandering in a week and a half, thanks be to grits!

Note to reader: The previous scene is so real, it's almost biblical.

Now, let's delve into this "grits are the perfect food" theory a little deeper. First of all let's explore the taste. There is none. And since there isn't any taste, I'm free to add in choice ingredients like chicken lips to give them a unique flavor; or I can choose to have them plain. If I have grits plain, I can imagine any taste I want. That's a decided benefit. On a mere whim, I can decide if they taste like a twice-baked potato or a fruit roll-up. Your imagination is a powerful thing, and you can use it to your healthful advantage when eating delicious grits.

Let's move on to grits' unmistakable aroma. Once again, there is none. When you smell nothing, you're smelling grits. Also, when you cook grits, nothing stinks up the kitchen. Well, that is until your kid comes home with that wet backpack that's full of week-old gym clothes and throws it on the floor. That would stink up your kitchen, but grits would never do that to you or your loved ones.

Next, we must acknowledge grits' superb texture. Have you ever wondered what it would be like to enjoy a warm, comforting, soothing bowl of sand? There ya go.

And speaking of bowls, grits are made to be eaten from a bowl. There is something very cool about eating from a bowl. Mankind has been doing it for generations. This amazing eat-from-a-bowl concept was started either by a small, savvy band of Asians in 7 B.C., or an enterprising country barber who had one too many tools.

CLETUS THE BARBER: Let's see. I've got two chairs, one clipper, and three bowls. What can I use this extra bowl for?

JUDY ANN: Cletus, time for breakfast!

CLETUS THE BARBER: That's it! I'll eat out of one of my tools!

Note to reader: The previous scene is so real, it's almost biblical.

And now we come to nutrition. Just one bowl of grits provides you with the yearly recommended allowance of carbs. One bowl. Now is that nutritional value or what?

"But sir," you say, "I'm an over-zealous health nut who drives everyone in my family crazy because I'm still on the outdated Atkins diet. My Atkins book says grits are inherently evil, and I even saw a news report on TV where Dr. Atkins called grits 'the fallen food.'"

Well, in response, let me say that he doesn't know what he's talking about. He's a doctor, not a chef. I guess Dr. Atkins doesn't know that "carbs" is short for "carburetors." Grits are a POWER food. Anybody ever call manna a POWER food? Next case on the docket, bailiff.

And lastly, or *finally* as you may be thinking, grits are extra filling. Eat a hearty bowl for breakfast every morning followed by drinking three tall glasses of water, and you'll be skipping lunch because your stomach is turning like a loaded concrete truck. That's a healthy lifestyle choice my friends.

A couple of follow-up points, if I may. There is no other food as versatile as grits. When I lived in Orlando, Florida, I discovered you can kill fire ants with grits. Just sprinkle uncooked grits on the fire ant mound and the workers will take them directly back to the queen. It's at this point she crushes their heads 'cause she wanted a cinnamon roll. Not everyone likes grits, including some fussy insects.

You can also use grits as an adhesive. You know that chair with the broken leg in your den? Let me tell you that cheese grits (instant only) make a great adhesive. Get a haircut bowl, put in two packs of instant cheese grits, add in a quart of three-day-old, room-temperature buttermilk, slap it in the microwave for 1:25, and you've got super glue that would adhere the space shuttle to the launch pad.

Note to reader: If you happen to be a teenager, don't get any ideas.

MUST-HEAR SERMON:

There's More Than One Way to Skin a Pastor Search Committee

Is manna really God's perfect food? Based on my painstaking research, detailed analysis and official Czechoslovakian government documentation, I would say no. And especially not when compared to the amazing, incredible grit. Take home a box today as I continue to look for Scriptural documentation to verify my half-baked hypothesis.

Note to reader: Tonight, remember this phrase: Grits—it's what's for dinner. ☺

chapter sixteen

TAX-FREE SHOPPING WEEKEND

"Only little people pay taxes."
—*Leona Helmsley*

Tennessee just had its first tax-free shopping weekend. It was held the weekend before school started; so a lot of people received breaks on clothes, computers, and chewing gum.

Most people I talked to said they loved it, thought it was a huge success, and that they ought to do something like this more often. And I can see the logic of a tax-free weekend for the citizens of our great state. But professional politicians, please don't stop there. Listen to the voice of the people, and the people say give us these other weekends as well:

Kid-free Weekend

This is when the state takes all the kids under the age of 18 and transports them via hot-air balloon to Dalton, Georgia—also known as The Carpet Capital of the Entire Solar System. Once across the state line, the kids will be contained on 4,248 acres of

Berber cut-pile carpeting. While the kiddies are romping, you're rolling with your new-found hours of freedom. Thanks, state of Tennessee.

Loud Obnoxious Person Talking on a Cell Phone-free Weekend

My personal favorite. This would be the weekend when you don't even come close to hearing another person's cell-phone conversation. And no one would dare use his cell phone that weekend because he would be fined a year's wages and imprisoned for up to 25 years. I know it's harsh, but it's the law. If you have a problem with it, simply build a bridge and get over it.

Doofus-free Weekend

A wonderful weekend when the state rounds up all the doofuses and makes them ride miniature horses to Smartt, Tennessee. Yes, the founder of Smartt was a doofus, as you can tell by his spelling of the town. I've actually been sent there three times; and every time I come home, my wife tells me how much she enjoyed the doofus-free weekend. I like helping her out like that.

Toilet Plunger-free Weekend

A true blessing. This would free up dads all across the state from having to plunge the commode. Actually, we could tie this into Taking the Garbage Out-free Weekend, too. Both seem to be a dad's inherent job, so why not give us a break from these two thankless tasks? No plunger and no garbage plus no whining from anyone equal a huge hit.

Work-free Week

After many late-night committee meetings, it was decided to expand on this one from a weekend to a week. The thought here is that when you show up at your place of employment, you just hang out for the week. You don't really do anything but talk to other people, catch up on your reading, and take two-hour lunches. And the best part is, you have free rein to surf the Internet as much as you like. Government employees are exempt from this because they already celebrate it quite extensively.

World War-free Weekend

I'd settle for a war-free 10 minutes. However, we have a better chance of rounding up every doofus in the state of Tennessee, putting them on miniature horses, and having them gallop off to a misspelled town than to stop every single war on this planet for even 30 seconds—let alone an entire weekend.

Calorie-free Weekend

This is the weekend the majority of people want to start off with. You can eat whatever you want, whenever you want it. Also, most folks prefer this weekend be positioned around Thanksgiving or Christmas for maximum effect. I like it as well, but I think you'd have to have an indigestion-free day to go along with it.

Apathy-free Weekend

A weekend where there is no indifference. Suddenly, everyone cares. All people show concern and interest for others and in all situations. There is a sense of helping out with great enthusiasm. Everyone pitches in without complaining. Every single person does his or her part to make this world a more loving and delightful place to exist. The "me-first" mentality is put on the shelf until Monday morning. People develop a keen awareness of the needs of people and then meet those needs in a cheerful and uplifting manner. And all people work with passion while keeping in the back of their minds who they are really serving.

Let's all be on the lookout for the needs of others; and then, when the opportunity presents itself, meet and fill those needs quickly.

In Romans 12:11, Paul encouraged us to, "Never be lacking in zeal, but keep your spiritual fervor, serving the Lord." It would be great if we did have an "Apathy-free Weekend," but that's not going to happen until we all get to Heaven. In the meanwhile, one thing we can do—on our own right now—is to serve the Lord through others by displaying passion and joy.

Let's all be on the lookout for the needs of others; and then, when the opportunity presents itself, meet and fill those needs quickly. Sometimes, you may run into a simple need, such as coming across someone who needs to laugh; and it's up to you to say just the right thing to get her to chuckle. Or maybe winter is around the corner, and you talk with a person who doesn't own a nice, heavy coat. So go ahead and purchase it for him.

Just don't be tempted like me to wait until the Tax-free Shopping Weekend to take him to the store. It's that sort of thinking that sends me riding off to the Doofus-free Weekend.

chapter seventeen

GROWING UP METHODIST

"I am not afraid that the people called
Methodists should ever cease to exist
either in Europe or America. But I am
afraid lest they should only exist as a
dead sect, having the form of religion
without the power. And this undoubt-
edly will be the case unless they hold
fast both the doctrine, spirit, and
discipline with which they first set out."
—*John Wesley*

I grew up Methodist. One fond memory that stays with me
is how many times we stood up and then sat back down during
church service. Seems like every two minutes they'd ask us to stand
up for 30 seconds, and then we'd sit back down for two minutes.
And then we'd do it all over again. Now that I look back, I don't
think all that up and down made me a better Christian; but it did
make me healthier.

Not only did I burn a ton of calories, but I made the high school deep-knee-bend team and was voted all-state twice. The cheerleaders were like, "Wow, you're awesomely good."

And without breaking stride while working out, I'd simply reply, "I'm Methodist."

I can remember looking over where most of the senior adults sat during the service. They'd get up one time; and after that, they weren't moving. They were smart. I used to bug my mom to let me pretend I was elderly, but she has this peculiar notion about family all sitting (and standing) together during worship.

I think the senior adults knew it was more like a combination church service and YMCA workout program. That could explain why Zelpha Naxly would always show up in sweat pants. She couldn't hear that well or see very far, but—bless her heart—she could do squats with the best of them.

You know how some churches are known as a "friendly" church or a "loving" church? We were known as a "cardiovascular" church. People would say, "You need to visit Bearden United Methodist; they'll increase your lung capacity." The downside was we scared off a lot of families because we made their children do trunk rotations in the vestibule.

We also did a lot of responsive readings. I can remember one Sunday when I was about 8 or 9, I asked my mom what a responsive reading was and she said, "That's when the pastor reads something out loud, and then we read something back out loud."

So I got out a comic book. The preacher read a passage from the hymnal, and I followed that with a passage between Archie and Jughead. Yet an early missed opportunity when a vow of silence would have served me well because that stunt got me taken out by my ear. In fact, I got taken out of church by my ears so many times that by the time I was a teenager, I looked like Spock from "Star Trek." Right before we'd walk into church, Dad would remind me, "Son, since you look like that space freak, try using your brain like him."

Actually Mom handled the discipline in church. She was tough. Sitting next to Mom was like worshiping God with Jaws at your side. I knew she was lurking; I just didn't know when she was going to hit the bait. And bait was my arms. I'd be methodically kicking the pew in front of me with my hard-shell Buster Brown shoes, and she would take a chunk out of my arm the size of a small block of cheese. To this day, I have craters on my arms that won't grow skin or hair.

If I happen to be wearing a short-sleeved shirt, and I'm sharing my faith with someone, they always ask, "What in the world is wrong with your arms?" I just have to remember *not* to say, "I got all these during church service. And by the way, would you like to go with me next Sunday?"

Oddly enough, I have yet to lead anyone to Christ. Maybe that's just the Methodist in me. ℮

MUST-HEAR SERMON:

Opportunity Knocks Once and Then Uses E-mail the Rest of the Time

chapter eighteen

BIBLE TRANSLATIONS

"Too often we see the
Bible through whatever
lens we get from our culture."
—*Brian McLaren*

You have to be careful when you read the different Bible translations that are available to the public. There are a lot of people out there who change the Bible into something that doesn't even come close to staying true to the original manuscripts.

I was in a non-denominational Christian bookstore, Bibles-A-Million, and they had Bible translations I didn't know even existed. There were over 128 different translations of the Bible. Among those were the ultra-contemporary translation, easy-to-read King James translation, giant-print translation, the phonetic translation, sci-fi translation, teens with attitude translation, the how-to translation, and the Louis L'Amour cowboy translation. That last one was a good read, I have to admit. I enjoyed learning about when Saint Paul had his posse hightailing it after Christians up to Damascus, and he yelled out, "Let's cut 'em off at the pass, boys!" That scene really brought the Bible to life for me.

So I decided to look through every translation to see if the meaning of a particular verse stayed true to the original manuscripts. I mean, how many ways can you interpret John 18:10? Apparently, there are 128 different ways you can say, "Then Simon Peter, who had a sword, drew it and struck the high priest's servant, cutting off his right ear."

Whatever translation you do decide
to use, study it with a passion and
find the gold nuggets that God
has given us through His Word.

Good Ol' Boy Translation: "Peter whipped out his buck knife and cut the ol' servant guy. Took his ear clean off. Wanna dip?"

Romance Novel Translation: "Tears welled deep from within the heart of Peter. He tried to hold back his conflicting emotions; but try as he must to appear stoic and manly, a small, caring tear shown as like the dew clinging to a fresh-cut blade of grass. Peter glanced downward once more; there laid the ear, glistening in the morning sun."

Children's Book from the 1960s: "Look, look. See Peter. See Peter use sword. See man looking for ear. Did Spot get ear? No. Did Fluffy get ear? No."

Children's Book from the 1990s: "If you give Peter a sheath, he'll want a sword to go with it. And if you give him a sword, he'll want to slash off somebody's ear. And if he slashes off somebody's ear, he'll want to go for the spleen next …"

Self-Help: "Peter brainstormed as he strategically developed his short- and long-term goals. Not to be overlooked were his daily affirmations encouraging him that he was a skillful swordsman: 'I'm good enough, I'm smart enough, and gosh darn it, I can cut an ear off.'"

Think this is way out? Not really. Some current translations on the shelves today have given the Bible a non-offensive, politically correct makeover. They are, in a sense, molding the Bible to the standards of today's culture. Shouldn't it be the other way around? All I'm really saying is, instead of using these trendy translations, look for a precise translation of the Bible that preserves the integrity of Scripture.

But whatever translation you do decide to use, study it with a passion and find the gold nuggets that God has given us through His Word. And for the record, gold nuggets were exactly what Saint Paul lost in the Louis L'Amour cowboy translation when his stagecoach was robbed near the coast of Malta. ☺

chapter nineteen

GULLIBLE LIKE GUMBO

"We think sometimes that poverty
is only being hungry, naked, and
homeless. The poverty of being
unwanted, unloved, and uncared
for is the greatest poverty."
—*Mother Teresa*

I had just given a keynote speech in Los Angeles, and I
was heading back to the hotel on foot when I was approached by
a street person. He had the look of a street person, and he had the
odor of a street person. His smell reminded me of an odd mixture
of my Uncle Harold's winter coat and an opened can of baked
beans. He had holes in his shoes, his face was dirty, and his clothes
looked to be a collection of discarded rags and yesterday's newspaper. I remember thinking, *In the hierarchy of homeless people,
this guy isn't even on the list.*

By both worldly and spiritual standards, he was the least of
the least. And the Holy Spirit brought this verse of Scripture from

Matthew to me where Jesus said, "… whatever you did for one of the least of these brothers of mine, you did for me" (25:40).

So I stopped, made eye contact, smiled and said hello. And he said, "Sir, I'm not going to lie to you. I am an evacuee of hurricane Katrina. Here's my card." He then presented me with a four-by-six-inch laminated card that said, "Official Louisiana Evacuee, Hurricane Katrina." That's what I love about America; even the displaced have business cards.

He said, "Sir, I haven't eaten in a couple of days, and I was wondering if you could spare some money so I can get something to eat."

I noticed we were standing a half-a-block away from a seafood restaurant. So I said, "Let's go inside that restaurant and I'll buy you whatever you want for dinner. In fact, I'll eat with you 'cause I'm hungry, too. By the way, do you like gumbo?"

He replied, "Don't know, never had it."

And he's hoping I'm gullible like the gumbo he's never had.

So I led the way down the street; and as we went up the steps to the restaurant, he started to slow down. As I opened the door to the restaurant, he paused, dropped his head, and said, "You know what I really need? I need money for bus fare so I can look for a job."

I looked at him, "But don't you want to eat?"

"Well, I need a job first," he said without lifting his head, "If you could just spare some money so I can find a job?"

I asked, "What about the gumbo?"

"I wouldn't like it," he flatly stated.

So it turns out he just wanted my money, but he didn't really want it for food—or bus fare.

And once again it came down to the question: Do you give street people money that you know they'll use for something that's not good for them like drugs, alcohol, or an *American Idol Greatest Covered Hits* CD? Do you help support their habits and in turn hurt them? My friend Ned from Akron (that's what's on his business card, "Ned from Akron") says he's never gotten the feeling that Jesus encouraged handouts to those who would misuse them.

I forget sometimes that no matter how
confusing, how much time it takes,
how irritating, or how tired and worn
out we are, we're here to serve Jesus.

He also says, "Your brain is smarter than you are; let it do its job."

Ned from Akron makes my brain think sometimes. So, let me ask you: What would your brain do? Would you give the street person a dollar or two? Would you give him some change out of your pockets? Would you take a vow of silence and just keep walking? Would you tell him you're no dummy and that you know he's lying to you? Would you say a silent prayer for him? Would you pray with him and then walk away? For this particular situation, is there a correct answer?

I forget sometimes that no matter how confusing, how much time it takes, how irritating, or how tired and worn out we are, we're here to serve Jesus. No matter what appearance He takes, we are here to serve Him as best we can in a positive and uplifting manner. But, do we serve Him by hurting Him?

So, what did I do? Well, you'd have to ask Ned from Akron's brain, which—based on his theory—is smarter than he is. ☉.

chapter twenty

I'M A WIMPY CHRISTIAN

"Move out of your comfort zone.
You can only grow if you are willing to
feel awkward and uncomfortable…"
—*Brian Tracy*

Sometimes I feel like I'm the biggest wimp of a Christian. And I feel especially like a whimpering flunky of a follower when I research and study the life of the Apostle Paul. Let's recount just a fraction of the things he went though while being obedient to Christ:

Five different times he was given 39 lashes with a whip. Three times he was just generally beaten with rods. He was stoned by angry people with a quarry full of rocks. He temporarily lost his sight. He was bitten by a poisonous snake, shipwrecked three times, lost at sea once, thrown in various jails and prisons where he was beaten and left without clothes, suffered from anxiety problems, and often he went hungry to the point of starvation. And, oh yeah, most folks also think he was eventually beheaded.

Now, let's tally up some of the things I've gone through while being obedient to Christ:

Countless nights I've slept on uncomfortable pillows in various three-star hotels in cities where I didn't know how to locate the closest Starbucks. Twenty-four times I've had flight delays of over an hour. I've had 12 actual cancellations of flights. I've lost my favorite luggage with brand-new toothbrush, disposable razor-blade, and expensive cholesterol medicine inside. I was in a New York City cab wreck where I suffered the mussing of my hair. I

You might not have to be shipwrecked, and you may not even have to sleep on a lumpy hotel bed; but look for ways to get out of your comfort zone for Christ.

---

had an ATM machine in Atlanta charge me $5 for a $20 fast-cash transaction. I've eaten numerous heavy pasta dinners late at night, throwing off my sensitive digestive system. I've suffered an eight-hour sinus blockage from moldy conference room carpet. My last name was mispronounced twice in front of a small audience of farmers in Peoria. Three times I've had to stop and ask directions from a complete stranger. And I once gave a keynote speech titled "The Pursuit of Holiness" while wearing women's socks. (They were my wife's socks as I packed the wrong pair for the trip.)

Maybe my wimpy-ness comes from wanting to stay in my Christian comfort zone. And I'm totally comfortable with that. But I wonder, *What could I accomplish for the Kingdom if I gave up some of my creature comforts? What if I gave up an hour of TV time for an hour of Bible research/study time? What if I gave up sleeping late for early prayer time?*

Look to people who you consider great or effective Christians, such as Paul, and see what they gave up in comfort and gained in Christ. You might not have to be shipwrecked, and you may not even have to sleep on a lumpy hotel bed; but look for ways to get out of your comfort zone for Christ. I have more to write on this subject, but I need to take a break and go adjust the thermostat. It's a little stuffy in here. ☉

chapter twenty-one

THANK YOU, MRS. CROSS

*"The MoonPie is...more than a
snack. It's a cultural artifact."
—William Ferris, Center for the
Study of Southern Culture*

My dad just sent me an e-mail. He wrote that Mrs. Cross
passed away today. She was 93. That's all I really knew her by, "Mrs.
Cross." The ironic thing was, she was anything but cross. Her real
name should have been Mrs. Smile or Mrs. Patient. Or even, Mrs.
MoonPie. Yes, that was her real name, Mrs. MoonPie.

Let me back up.

When I was a second grader, Mrs. Cross came to our house once
a week to help with the cleaning and ironing. She usually came on
Thursdays. One morning I wasn't feeling well, and it just happened
to be on a Thursday; so Mom let me stay home from school. All
that morning I followed Mrs. Cross around the house. She talked
to me, and she would laugh and smile as she went about her
chores. She really didn't care that I was underfoot; or if she did, she
didn't show it.

When it came time for lunch, Mrs. Cross asked me if I wanted her dessert. It was a MoonPie. I don't recall having had a MoonPie up to that point in my life; but it sounded good, so I gladly took it from her. It was also quite by accident, or maybe intelligent design, that I was drinking an RC Cola at the time. That wonderful combination of solid and liquid processed sugar (it's known throughout the Southland as the "sixth" food group) would become a staple of my diet for the next 20 years.

That day, I knew that I must have a MoonPie again. But I had no money to purchase one, so I devised a straightforward plan. I would be sick every Thursday! Simple in its brilliance, I paraded around the house, my arms raised in the air, "I have beaten the system, and I'm only 7!"

The next Thursday morning rolled around, and I jumped out of bed with great excitement and told my mom that I had a sore throat and a raspy cough and that my fingers even hurt a little. With great conviction, I demonstrated to her all my ailments, acting them out as if I had an Oscar nomination on the line.

Unbelievably, Mom bought it. So I sat in my pajamas and waited. I waited for Mrs. Cross and her brown paper sack. When she arrived, I followed her all over the house as we talked and smiled and laughed until lunch time. Once again she offered me her only MoonPie; and, once again, I ate it with great delight. As I savored the last incomparable crumb and downed the final drop of the sweet RC Cola, I can remember thinking, *This is Heaven, and it happens on Thursday.*

The following Thursday morning I had preplanned a tummy issue. I went to Mom, hands over my stomach, eyes toward the ground, and moaning, "My tummy *hurts.*"

"Greater love has no one than this; that a person lay down her MoonPies for her friends."

Mom gave me "the look" and—in a no-nonsense fashion—directly carted me off to school. It was the worst day of my young life, knowing that at noon I would be sitting in class while Mrs. Cross would be sitting in my kitchen.

By the time I reached home that afternoon, I had forgotten all about it being Thursday. As I ran into the back of the house through the kitchen door, the first thing I noticed there, next to the sink, on the sparkling kitchen counter, protected in a shiny, cellophane wrapper was a single, glorious MoonPie.

Jesus said in John 15:13 that, "Greater love has no one than this, that he lay down his life for his friends." I think my translation might read, "Greater love has no one than this, that a person lay down her MoonPies for her friends."

Thank you, Mrs. Cross, that you loved me enough to give up your dessert for me. And I know you're in Heaven right now, but I just wanted to let you know that today is Tuesday. So in two days, on Thursday morning, I'll wake up and tell my wife I have a sore throat and a raspy cough and that my fingers even hurt a little. And

I'll stay home and won't do any work at all. And I'll smile, and I'll laugh, and I'll be patient…and for lunch, I'll savor a single Moon-Pie and think of a wonderful, beautiful lady named Mrs. Cross. ☺

chapter twenty-two

IT'S HARD TO BE HUMBLE WHEN YOU HIT A GOLF BALL 325 YARDS

"Humility is like underwear,
essential, but indecent if it shows."
—*Helen Nielsen*

One area of my life in which I struggle is being humble. Now, I make a mental effort to walk in humbleness; and for most of the time, I can—sort of—do exactly that. But there are those few occasions where I just puff up and make a real jerk out of myself. Golfing would be a perfect opportunity for me to practice a vow of silence. But I just love to talk trash after a well-hit ball.

Now keep in mind, I'm a horrid golfer. And the game of golf humiliates me for much of the 18 holes, but there's always that rare occasion where I step up on the tee box and accidentally connect with the ball and drive it solidly down the middle for over 325 yards.

When that happens, watch out playing partners. The first thing I do is drop my club to the ground and make a series of quick muscle poses like Mr. Olympia on a lunch-hour photo shoot. Then I talk some trash: "Crunched it, *ladies!* That was a seven iron if you want to note it on your scorecard."

When I walk/gloat up to the ball, it's a mere 15 yards off the green. Then, as all eyes are on me, I awkwardly stab my club into the ground, muffing the shot. It rolls 13 inches. Guffaws and snorts from my partners. But I don't care. You see, I'm still living off that 325-yard drive. (I really think it went 327, actually.)

Next shot, I hit it thin and blade it over the green into a bunker. Two tries to get out of the sand, and then my normal three-putt, and it's a triple bogie on my scorecard. By the way, I stop and pick up the ball the moment I reach three over par. I have a doctor's note that says it's OK because of my fluctuating self-esteem levels.

MUST-HEAR SERMON:

It's Not Whether You Win or Lose, but How Many Red Lights You Can Beat on the Way Home

Sadly, it's always like that when I'm involved in any type of competition. Like when I'm playing cards with my retired Baptist preacher father-in-law. (There is no exchange of money going on, folks, just bragging rights.) But old Preacher Joe is pretty solid at the game of Rook; so when I happen to beat him, I tell him about it so there's no mistaking who is the winner of a particular game.

It's really pathetic that in the morning I could be doing something like leading a prison Bible study; and that night while playing cards, I take the kitty, plus the Bird, plus all the trumps, and set my competition in the hole to win the game. And I'll jump up with the finger-pointing and in-your-face verbal jabs, "Crunched it, *ladies*! That was a seven iron if you want to note it on your scorecard."

I know; I need to work on my trash talk. But when you're humble like me, anything you say when you win will work. It's the *tone* behind the words that drives everyone nuts.

However, I think I could really stand to actually practice some solid New Testament teachings. Like in Philippians 2:3 Paul stated, "… in humility consider others better than yourselves."

And so, for the next 21 days I'm going to consider that everyone I run into is better than me. And I'll make a choice to serve them in such a manner. Unless, of course, I happen to be out playing golf. That would be asking too much. ℮

chapter twenty-three

LESSON LEARNED

"Therefore, holy brothers, who share
in the heavenly calling, fix your
thoughts on Jesus, the apostle and
high priest whom we confess."
—*Hebrews 3:1*

I was flying up the coast from California to Alaska early one
morning, and I was fortunate enough to have a window seat looking
out over the Pacific. The view both enthralled and reminded me of
the splendor of God's majestic hand. The ocean was a shimmering
crystal of blue that stretched out for miles; but it was the unusual
grouping of small, puffy, white clouds that held my attention.

As far as I could see there were hundreds of thousands of single,
oval-shaped clouds in tight formation. They looked strangely like
an army of Q-tips heading south. My first thought was, "They must
be heading to Oakland." I know a lot of cities in America could use
a good cleaning, but Oakland needs a major swabbing. And I only

say this because if you've seen how some of the Oakland Raider football fans dress for a game, unsightly ear wax comes to mind.

The flight attendant brought me back to reality when she rolled the beverage cart next to my seat and presented me with a cup of lukewarm coffee. Later, as I turned my gaze back toward the incredible sight of sun, clouds, and ocean, God's splendor and majesty once again overtook me. Strangely, it was in the midst of this incredibly deep and nurturing spiritual moment that I suddenly felt the odd sensation of wet socks. I looked down, almost expecting to witness Jesus washing my feet; but instead, I saw a steady stream of apple juice cascading down from the seat in front of me and onto my socks and shoes.

I quickly stood up and leaned over the seat to witness a sleeping child. His mother was next to him, reading a magazine about productive parenting; so I said to her in the most caring of tones, "I believe your son spilled his apple juice. It's running through the seats and onto my shoes and socks."

To which the mom replied, "Tyler doesn't drink apple juice."

This is what theologians call an "Uh-oh moment." And not only did I have an "Uh-oh moment," so did the mom, the kid, and the flight attendant who helped usher the soaked kid to the bathroom. And as the little boy sleepily walked past my seat, I noticed he was wearing a black and silver sweatshirt with a logo stamped right on the front reading, "Oakland Raiders."

I sat back down, realizing I just experienced yet another "Uh-oh moment": *What if God is a Raiders fan? What if He is playing a practical joke on me for disrespecting His team? Or what if He is gently instructing me not to compare an entire American city to unsightly ear wax?*

You just never know when you might encounter a kid with a weak bladder— or God when He's in a playful mood.

So I encourage all of us, especially me, to do a better job of monitoring our thoughts at all times because you just never know when you might encounter a kid with a weak bladder—or God when He's in a playful mood. ☺

chapter twenty-four

ON GOD, GOLF, AND GUITAR

"For God did not give us a spirit of
timidity, but a spirit of power, of
love and of self-discipline."
—*2 Timothy 1:7*

I think God, golf, and guitar are a lot alike; especially when
it comes to struggling to master these three disciplines. For instance
in golf, I've seen people cuss and break their clubs when they
become frustrated. At a rock concert, I've seen musicians cuss,
spit fake chicken blood, and break their guitars.

I also witnessed a man use profane language and throw his
Bible. Actually, that man was me. My older brother had died
suddenly and unexpectedly, and I was pretty mad at God. Now,
I didn't cuss *at* God. *(NOTE TO EDITOR: Being a Christian-themed
book, I'm not sure if it's OK to write about cussing and God in
the same paragraph. You might want to take this out in the final
edit. Thanks.)* But I was just cussing and spitting in the most
general sense, and I'll admit that. I also threw my Bible like a
worthless putter after a missed two-foot putt for birdie. Yes, it was

a dastardly moment in my life and one that I'm not proud of in the least.

But like those who work on their golf games or their guitar riffs, I went back to working on making my relationship with God better. Now, I know I'll never be perfect at any of these three disciplines. And yes, I do think God is a discipline. After all, God is love.

Think about it. Most great golfers and guitarists tend to practice daily. That's a discipline. And when they're not practicing or playing, they're talking about it. And when they're not talking about it, they're thinking about it. And when they're not thinking about it, they're asleep and dreaming about it. One more thing about practicing golf: On your downswing, keep your hands next to your pants pocket. If this tip helps you, send me a handwritten thank-you card along with $10 cash. *(NOTE TO EDITOR: Is this legal—getting money for golf tips in a book about how to have a more meaningful Christian walk? You probably ought to take this out in the final edit. Thanks.)*

So how do you practice being in and with God/love? Well, I look to Jesus, and I practice some of the behaviors He displayed. Most I'm not very good at.

For instance, I repeatedly tried walking on water at the indoor YMCA pool. But the lifeguards escorted me out because I disrupted the senior citizens' kick 'n' float class. I tried feeding 5,000 people, but the closest I came was helping to feed 42 during a spaghetti dinner for the homeless. I was in charge of bread. Maybe one day I'll work my way up to salads. *(NOTE TO EDITOR: What I really want to do is be in charge of meatballs; but that sounds preten-tious, doesn't it? Please take this out in the final edit. Thanks.)*

I also tried making some sick people feel better. But with HIPPA laws the way they are, healing people becomes problematic. I mean, if I can't get personal information from total strangers, how can I expect to help them? I always tell them, "If you don't give me your background information along with a credit card number, there's nothing I can do." Besides, I have no formalized medical training, unless you count when I took a first-aid class during my fourth year of junior college.

Now my dad (who often turns water into milk by using city tap water and freeze-dried powered milk crystals) said I should attempt to turn water into wine. He gave me some excellent tips, but the closest I could get was something that looked like a weak strain of grape juice.

So OK, I can't practice the big things Jesus did, but I can sure practice the little things He did. Like in guitar, you practice your scales. It's such a basic thing, but I know a lot of average guitar-ists who don't practice the little things like scales. They jump right into the excitement of playing; but because they ignore the basics, they remain average guitarists. *(NOTE TO EDITOR: I don't really practice my scales, I just crank the amp up and let 'er rip. Now, that's fun. Please take this out in the final edit. Thanks).*

In golf you practice the little things like getting to the course on time so you can work on your short game, like putting and chip-ping. And then you casually walk over to the driving range and work on your pitch shots and short irons. A lot of golfers I play with just rush out to the number one tee box and begin whaling away with mulligans and do-overs. *(NOTE TO EDITOR: I would like to work on my short game before a round, but who has time? Not me. Hey, do me a favor and please take this out in the final edit. Thanks.)*

So how do you practice the small things when it comes to the discipline of God? First thing you do is love all the time. You can also get out of bed while it's still dark. Then you have a daily I-will-not-break-this-commitment-no-matter-how-groggy-I-am prayer time and Bible study period for at least two hours. Follow that with fifteen minutes of vocal praise and end the session with a classic hymn of your choice sung out on your back porch. *(NOTE TO EDITOR: You know the drill.)*

Practice the small disciplines in your car. On your morning commute, practice letting others in front of you without expecting a thank-you wave in return. Practice not racing so you can beat a yellow light before it turns red. ("It was orange, officer. The light was just going from yellow to red, but it was still orange.")

Practice the small disciplines at work. When you're on the phone with a difficult client or vendor, silently pray for him or her and listen for the Holy Spirit to guide you through the conversation. Remember to thank God and praise Him when you're stressed because that's when you need His loving arms the most.

Like golf and guitar, practicing the discipline of God takes daily commitment and a willingness to do the small things when serving others. *(NOTE TO EDITOR: I think I'll actually try some of this stuff in a couple of weeks. It sounds like it might be practical and help-ful. Please take this out in the final edit. Thanks.)* ☺

MUST-HEAR SERMON:

Carpe Diem and Identifying Other Species of Christian Life

chapter twenty-five

ROOSTER BOOSTER

"We do chicken right."
—*KFC*

Romans 12:2 says: "Do not conform any longer to the pattern of this world, but be transformed by the renewing of your mind."

When you're working on renewing your mind, it's helpful to be reminded that you have an active part in the process. So I look around at things in life to see who is renewing what. Who is looking at things in new or even creative ways?

I watch a little of Discovery Channel on TV, and I figured out that NASA uses the renewing-of-the-mind principle. They constantly renew the way they think about methods to solve space flight problems. Such as, they actually take parts of the space shuttle and shoot them with nine-pound chickens.

That's a new way of using dinner.

I know you think I make half of this stuff up (it's more like two-thirds); but they really, truly take an unplucked chicken—thawed not frozen—and shoot it out of a naval cannon at 300 miles-per-hour into a windshield or side panel of the space shuttle to test space flight durability.

This leads me to ask: Are there barnyards in space? Did Buzz Lightyear have a near miss with a chicken coop? I thought asteroid fields were dangerous. I guess instead it's Old MacDonald's Farm.

SHUTTLE COMMANDER: Houston, we have a…cluck, cluck here; and a cluck, cluck, there.

COMMAND CENTRAL: Here a cluck and there a cluck. Is everywhere a cluck, cluck?

SHUTTLE COMMANDER: Well of course!

COMMAND CENTRAL: Then bring us back a party tray of nuggets.

So how did NASA develop this idea? The answer is they had to look at solving problems in a completely different way. Or, one of their scientists was driving around town and got the idea when he saw a Chick-fil-A cow writing on a billboard, "Shoot more chickens." I think that last explanation works just fine for me.

This is a real NASA program, folks. I have actually visited one of the testing sites here in Tennessee. It's at the Arnold Air Force Base and Feed Store. Arnold's is the largest flight simulation and poultry projectile facility in the world. They have over 50 wind tunnels located in their Foghorn Leghorn sector (that's a joke, son; I say, ah, that's a joke) of the base. They also have three acres of dead-but-still-feathered chickens, and they have one active naval cannon called "The Rooster Booster." I think the name doesn't really fit because they only shoot hens out of the cannon, not roosters. But you know the old saying, "That's close enough for government work."

NASA also has a name for this outrageous program. They call it the Scientific Poultry Launching Assessment Test. But, once again, you know the government, they can't live without acronyms; so for short, they call it S.P.L.A.T.

Renewed thinking—it can be messy.

But making an effort to look at things in a different light can also open your mind to fresh possibilities for becoming the person you were intended to be. Let's say you have one person at work who just really drives you crazy. He knows where your hot buttons are and knows exactly when to push them. One way to deal with this in a fresh manner is to change the way you interpret his rude behavior because it's your interpretation of events that leads to your feelings and emotions. That particular person doesn't make you mad. You do, by your interpretation.

How can you change your interpretation of being brow-beaten or disrespected or made to feel inferior by someone? You forego your ego and study specific spiritual truths so deeply they actually become a part of who you are. Look to verses in the Bible such as Luke 6:22: "Blessed are you when men hate you, when

MUST-HEAR SERMON:

People Who Live in Glass Houses Shouldn't Throw Stones or Take Showers

they exclude you and insult you," or 1 Peter 3:9: "Do not repay evil with evil or insult with insult, but with blessing, because to this you were called so that you may inherit a blessing."

Renewed thinking says we're blessed when people push our hot buttons or give us verbal grief. And we might even be blessed when someone shoots a chicken out of a cannon... ☙

chapter twenty-six

STAPLED STOMACH

"There's a rumor going around that the
reason Kirstie Alley lost so much weight
was because she had her stomach
stapled. When asked about it, Alley
said, 'That's ridiculous. I didn't have
it stapled. I had it spot-welded.'"
—*Conan O'Brien*

People do all kinds of things when it comes to managing
their weight. And I always support them, encourage them, and
offer them advice while being oblivious that their issue is the same
thing I'm struggling with. Or maybe I just don't want to admit I have
weight problems, and I really just don't want to face dealing with it.

For instance, to lose a lot of weight fast, my obese uncle told
me he was going to have his stomach stapled. So at that point I
didn't think that maybe I should lose weight for health reasons, I
thought, "Stomach stapled? Sounds like something you could do
at work—cool!"

HUNGRY UNCLE: Bill, I need to drop a few pounds in a hurry. Could you staple my stomach here in the cubicle? Just use that new Swingline 2400 on me.

BODACIOUS BILL: Right after I fax off this gallbladder for Mr. Anderson, I'd be glad to.

So the family showed up at the hospital to hang out in the waiting room, and we started getting hungry. Somebody offered to make a food run. And I was like, "Just get me something simple like a quadruple-bacon-double-cheeseburger with a twice-loaded baked potato. And if they don't have that, get me something healthy. Just make sure it's saturated in fat."

My uncle was in there suffering for his eating habits, and I was supporting him by making sure animal fat permanently sealed off my arteries. And I noticed the women in my family were kind of sneaky with their orders, "I'll just have a small garden salad." And then in a hushed whisper they added, "With fried chicken strips and four ranch dressings and a double order of croutons." And then they announced for the whole waiting room to hear, "And put the dressing on the *side*."

We had a family member lying on an operating table, paying for years of bad eating habits, and we were pretending we were ordering dinner from Emeril. And the weird thing was, right after we got our food, we received word that things had turned serious. One of the doctors came out and told us, "I'm sorry to tell you this, but there's no marinara with the cheese sticks. And I had plainly ordered marinara."

Actually, things really did turn sort of serious as the doctors kind of botched the surgery, and my uncle had to stay in intensive care all night. So we all spent the night, and then the next morning a cousin got us all together and said, "Folks, we need to look in the mirror because this is a wake-up call." And we all agreed that it was.

"Do you not know that your body is a temple of the Holy Spirit, who is in you, whom you have received from God? You are not your own; you were bought at a price. Therefore honor God with your body." —1 Corinthians 6:19-20

And then he said, "Now does anybody care if I have that last doughnut?" And before anyone could say anything, the most Christian one of us out of the bunch decided we should save it for our uncle when they let him out of the hospital. And we all agreed to that, too, mainly because it was a raspberry-filled doughnut; and most folks really don't like those.

But this whole letting your body go and then doing something radical to fix it made me want to search the Scriptures to find out if there was anything about controlling your appetite. I came up with a few verses, but the passage that really hit me was 1 Corinthians 6:19-20, "Do you not know that your body is a temple of the Holy

Spirit, who is in you, whom you have received from God? You are not your own; you were bought at a price. Therefore honor God with your body."

Wow. That verse nails it. So my take-away lesson is that there will be no need for office-supply surgery if I memorize this Scripture. However, the next time I'm faced with a dozen hot, glazed Krispy Kreme doughnuts in my Sunday School class, I'll have to try to actually apply this verse. I'll let you know how it turns out. ☉

chapter twenty-seven

TENNIS BALL ON A STICK

"Simplicity is the ultimate sophistication."
—*Leonardo DaVinci*

I wonder if God wants us to be simple Christians

using simple methods to love and instruct while on our earthly mission. Sometimes I think simple is the best.

I was sitting in a mall somewhere in America, when I noticed workers cleaning scuff marks off the tile flooring. And they were using a very simple tool: a tennis ball attached to a stick. You would think they would use an electric buffer or a mop of some type, but it was a tennis ball attached to a long, wooden stick. And with just a slight rubbing, the marks would come right up.

But I had to wonder, *How did someone think up this tool? Who developed it? By what process was the tennis ball on a stick designed and developed? And who do you look for when hiring to use this simple-but-effective tool? Did the people have to interview for this job?*

FUTURE BOSS: So what are your qualifications?

RECENT GRAD: I graduated with a degree from Pine Sol University in Unusual Cleaning Management. My area of concentration was tennis ball on a stick, but I'm also very proficient at using football on a rope.

FUTURE BOSS: Excellent. Did you happen to gain any experience with toupee on a coat hanger?

RECENT GRAD: Yes, it's actually one of my favorites. It works great on those hard-to-reach places.

FUTURE BOSS: You can start right now, I'm taking a vacation.

I wonder if God wants us to be simple Christians using simple methods to love and instruct while on our earthly mission. Sometimes I think simple is the best.

I'm really amazed. With all the technology available to us right now—with all the billions of dollars invested in cleaning solutions—the most efficient way to clean miles of mall flooring is using a tennis ball on a stick.

So what does the Bible have to say about this? Apparently nothing; but I do encourage you to enjoy a more simple walk through life. Oh, and by the way, men, don't go out in your yard and get the dog's tennis ball and duct tape it to the end of a tree branch to clean the kitchen floor. Get a new tennis ball from the athletic shop and a five-foot wooden dowel from the hardware store. The Mrs. will simply be amazed and delighted with your proactive ingenuity. Yeah, I know. I'm a genius with an IQ that scores consistently over 98. ☺

chapter twenty-eight

THE HORRORS OF HUFFINESS

Jon: I think you'll like flying, Garfield. It's
a smooth, comfortable mode of travel.
[Garfield holds up an air-sickness bag]
Garfield: Then what are these little
bags for? The Easter egg hunt?
—*"Garfield in Paradise"*

I get tired of everything related to air travel. From delays
over lotion in someone's carry-on bag, to last-minute canceled
flights, to making an effort to love and understand people sitting
next to you who seem to enjoy garlic and onions but not underarm
deodorant; air travel is getting old.

I was flying from Tucson to Salt Lake City when I had a sudden
revelation. I was, at that very moment, to write a song about serving grits at every meal to the residents of a criminal insane asylum.
(I smell a hit.) However, I didn't have anything to capture my lyrics
on. So I got creative and looked through the seatback pocket and
found an air-sickness bag. Perfect. Air-sickness bags are almost all
white; and they don't have logos or printed instructions, so there's
a lot of space on which to write.

So I was jotting down these soon-to-be-in-my-mind-award-winning song lyrics, and the lady sitting next to me started making what I can only describe as a disgruntled huffing sound. It was the kind of sound that I assume a bear makes when, after much digging and clawing, he can't find a sarsaparilla root to eat.

So I looked at her, first of all to see if someone actually might have let a wild animal onto the plane (with Southwest you never know); and she declared, out loud, for the entire plane to hear, "You're taking notes on a *barf bag*?"

"I know, look at all this white space! It's great!" I exclaimed.

Increased displeasured huffing and puffing as she bellowed out, "But what does it say about the *quality* of your writing?"

And in the most loving, accepting, Christ-centered tone I could muster, I quipped, "It says that I'm good at regurgitating words."

Delayed fake smile from me, one final, loud exhale from her; and the battle was over. But I must tell you that I've felt really badly about that encounter from time to time. And it's not because I should have ignored her in the first place, And it's not because I wasn't successful with my vow of silence and gave her an off-the-cuff, smart-aleck answer. It's because I didn't tell her she made it into the chorus of my grits/insane asylum song. ☺

MUST-HEAR SERMON:

If It Walks Like a Duck, Quacks Like a Duck, and Looks Like a Duck, You Could Be Looking at an Opossum in Drag

chapter twenty-nine

DILUTING GOD

"I gave in, and admitted God was God."
—C.S. Lewis

You see on the television news people getting upset because America seems to be doing its best to take God out of our lives. Things like prayer in school, The Ten Commandments plaque at city hall, and the Christmas tree with the star on top in the middle of town square have all been removed. And that makes some Christians mad, but it makes other Christians want to join the party.

Here on the home front, the Presbyterian Church is doing its part to officially take God out of its members' lives. Denominational leaders are replacing the phrase "Father, Son, and Holy Spirit" with some very ambiguous names. They want their churchgoers to refer to God as a genderless spirit, among other things.

One of the names approved for God is *Rainbow of Promise*. And actually I have to stop here and scratch my head because I have no idea what that really means. Are we to pray to the *Rainbow of Promise* and then look for our own personal pot of gold at the end of said *Rainbow*? What's to stop us from calling the Holy Trinity *Star Light, Star Bright, First Star I See Tonight*? It works just as well as *Rainbow of Promise*.

Other names approved to replace God, Jesus, and the Holy Spirit are: *Storm that Melts Mountains, Life-giving Womb,* and *Overflowing Font. Overflowing Font?* On my Microsoft Word tool-bar I have over 43 fonts from which to choose. Is that what they're talking about? Sorry, but I'm not serving Arial, Times New Roman, or Cuckoo. Am I to lift my hands in the air in praise of Bookman Old Style or Verdana? It's very confusing.

But the most confusing thing they want the members to call our Father in Heaven is *Compassionate Mother*. No wonder church enrollment is dropping all over America; we don't know who we're worshiping.

However, being of optimistic spirit, I do see what could be a positive from changing God's name to something entirely vague. Let's say this trend catches on not only in here in the U.S.A. but all over the world. And let's say that other religions decide to follow suit with the name changes. Can you imagine if militant Muslims decided to call Allah something kind of random?

"Praise be the *Grain of Sand that Blends!*"

"You expect me to strap this bomb around my midsection in the name of the *Grain of Sand that Blends?*"

"Um, sure. Why not?"

"Here, *you* put this thing on. I'm gonna go build a Habitat for Humanity house."

I really don't think most folks would blow themselves up for the *Grain of Sand that Blends*. But you know people, it doesn't take much for us to bring about destruction and death. And in human terms, Christians and non-Christians alike can do a lot of things to make God sort of disappear. But that's just on the surface. What some fail to realize is that no matter what names are created for Him, God will never be diluted. Love will never be diluted. Truth will never be diluted. And Spirit will live on forever.

What some fail to realize is that no matter what names are created for Him, God will never be diluted.

I'd like to leave you with a couple of verses to meditate on for the next few days. The first one is John 4:24: "God is spirit, and his worshipers must worship in spirit and in truth."

And think on 1 John 4:16, my favorite verse ever: "God is love. Whoever lives in love lives in God." Or, if you prefer, we could change it up for a more politically correct, non-offensive read, "God is *Storm that melts Mountains*. Whoever lives in *Storm that melts Mountains* lives in God." That should provide some deep, spiritual inspiration for the masses. ☉

chapter thirty

THE MORMIST

"Religious experiences which are
as real as life to some may be
incomprehensible to others."
—*William O. Douglas*

I was giving a corporate seminar in downtown Salt Lake
City, Utah, and during my lunch break I decided to walk over and
visit the temple grounds with my fellow seminar leader and friend
Arnold "Dead Man Shoes" Fripplewipe. He got the nickname
Dead Man Shoes because he always complains that his shoes are
killing him. However, I think Stink Man Shoes might be a more
accurate description.

That said about Dead Man, we arrived at the temple wall and
just walked on in through the gate as pretty as you please; no waiting in line, no getting tickets, no registering for an extra wife. Less
than six feet in, however, we were greeted by two young, bright,
and cheerful tour guides—or as Dead Man calls them, "recruiting
coordinators."

"Welcome to the temple! Would you like us to show you the historic grounds?" they asked in the friendliest of unison tones.

And here's where it gets kind of squirrelly. You see, we really didn't want a sales pitch during our lunch hour. We just wanted to walk around on our own and take in the architecture; so—at the exact same time—I answered, "No thanks, we're not Mormon," and Dead Man said, "No thanks, we're just tourists." Unfortunately, our words meshed in the listeners' ears and came out as, "No thanks, we're Mormists."

The more Osmond-looking one out of the two said, "Excuse me?"

So I said, in all seriousness, "We're Mormist. We're half-Mormon and half-tourist. You know, Mormist. We're a splinter group."

The recruiting coordinators looked confused, and I was reminded of a universal principle: People won't bother you anymore when you baffle them with absurd statements. And with that, the more Osmond-looking one out of the two smiled "a little bit country" grin and flagged us on through to explore the grounds on our own. Or so we thought. Every time we walked past a tree or park bench, I would hear the whir of what sounded like a hidden security video camera turning to follow our every step. I was just about to tell Dead Man I was feeling freaked out when he said, "We just invented a new religion, you know."

"Huh?" I countered. By the way, "Huh?" is my best counter and seems to work well with my better half. However, police officers don't buy it.

Dead Man grabbed me by my arm, "The Mormist religion—we just invented it. You know how in that TV commercial a few years ago when somebody accidentally mixed his chocolate in with somebody else's peanut butter? And they got a totally new food group?"

"Huh?" I countered again because the first one really didn't work.

"You mixed your 'Mormon' in with my 'tourist,' and we got 'Mormist,'" smiled Dead Man.

"But I'm not in the Latter-day Saints and neither are you. I'm Southern Baptist, and you're Church of Christ," I protested.

"Doesn't matter," Dead Man stated. "We've developed an exciting new religion by accident, and I think we should go ahead right now and set up the belief system and bylaws."

Sounded cool to me, so here's what we came up with.

As a people who are half Mormon and half tourist, we believe in the following:

• Liberal use of sunscreen in places we can't talk about.

• The baptism of the beach ball, both inflated and deflated. Don't want to leave deflated beach balls out. Plus, we just might OK the baptizing of lawn darts or "jarts" as Dead Man calls them. We want to be open-minded about such matters, considering things you might take on vacation.

• Every member must know and use the secret handshake, footshake, and head-shake to identify other members. Just imagine getting 50 Mormists in a room and having them introduce themselves. It'd be like somebody put on a James Brown CD.

• Every member in good standing must go on a two-year mission to Universal Studios Florida or Gator-Rama Louisiana.

It's your choice as long as you bring us back a T-shirt and refrigerator magnet.

• Every Wednesday afternoon members must jump up and down on a sofa like Tom Cruise. (I know Tom isn't LDS, but more like LSD. However, we think sofa-jumping is quite centering and nurturing.)

We didn't get any further on our belief system and bylaws because Tom Cruise got me thinking about Scientology, and Dead Man didn't like that. "You don't mix Mormistism and Scientology; that's like mixing NASCAR with advertising," he complained.

I gave him a blank look, "NASCAR *is* advertising."

He poked a stiff finger in my chest, "We want to be a *pure* strain of Mormist!"

I told Dead Man he'd been out in the sun for too long, so we decided to head back to finish our seminar. Unfortunately for me, on the way back Dead Man had to stop and tell everyone he saw about the beauty of Mormistism. It was sort of embarrassing actually, but somehow we managed to pick up a pair of new converts and a $25 donation to help with our foreign mission trip to Gulf Shores, Alabama. ℗

MUST-HEAR SERMON:

A Watched Pot Never Gets Over Feeling Paranoid

chapter thirty-one

VAPOR LOCK IN THE LORD

"The proof of spiritual maturity is not
how pure you are but awareness
of your impurity. That very awareness opens the door to grace."
—*Phillip Yancey*

Last night I dreamt I was riding in a cab. (Thanks Lord, for that comfortable and clean-smelling mode of transportation.) And, without warning, the cab came to a screeching halt. The driver yelled out, "It's vapor lock, it's vapor lock!" And I said, "Oh no. Not vapor lock! Uh, what is that anyway?"

And the driver turned and gave me the "You dummy" look, so I said, "I bet there's some type of vapor in the engine, and it caused something to lock up." And the driver gave me a bigger "You dummy" look; and at that point, I woke up because he was starting to remind me of my wife.

I quickly wrote down the dream as best I could remember, and I asked the Lord to show me the meaning. But I didn't have time to wait around on Him, so I did the next best thing to praying and listening to God: I jumped online for the answer. What I found after my Internet search is that "vapor lock" is when a pocket of gasoline mist inside a carburetor or fuel pump—which some people call the "heart" of the car—stops the normal flow of gas and shuts the engine down.

And I suddenly remembered a car I had when I was 20 that suffered from terminal vapor lock. It would stall and then stop anytime I drove it for over 30 minutes. My friends—I'm sorry—my *friend* would never want to go anywhere with me: "Tim, I want to stay out later than a half-hour tonight," he would say.

I told him, "If you can't do something in 30 minutes or less, then there's no need in doing it at all."

Anyway, back to my junker. Once the car stopped, the only way to start it again was to sit there and wait while the engine cooled off. And once it did cool off, I could start it up and drive for another 30 minutes. I went across town once, and it took three hours. Boy, those were the days.

Back to my dream. It made me start thinking, and that's not a good thing because usually I set off smoke alarms. But I do wonder: When I can't feel the presence of the Lord in my heart, am I experiencing some sort of spiritual vapor lock? Maybe my heart is not as clean and pure as it needs to be to listen to the guidance of the Holy Spirit and so I stop operating like I was built to operate, spiritually speaking of course.

So from now on, to get back to being in synch with the Holy Spirit, I'll know to sit and wait on the Lord. Psalm 37:7 says, "Be still before the Lord and wait patiently for him."

Be still. Wait. Be patient. Who's got time for that? I guess I do if I'm not tuned up and running properly. But, come on people, it's a hard thing to do to be still before the Lord and wait with patience.

We've got lives to live. We've got committee meetings to attend. (Well, I don't, thank goodness.) We've got church-league softball games, where a good fight is always waiting to break out.

I do wonder: When I can't feel the presence of the Lord in my heart, am I experiencing some sort of spiritual vapor lock?

Did I mention careers, kids, or pets? What about chores? Somebody has to go to the grocery store because there is absolutely nothing in the house for dinner. Or should we eat out? Yeah, let's go fight restaurant crowds for a healthy, relaxing meal. And then we can stop at Wal-Mart and pick up a few things on the way home.

No wonder we experience vapor lock in the Lord. Our lives are turning into something that actually stresses us out and tends to shut down our spiritual growth.

So let's get back up and running again like the finely tuned Christian machines we were created to be. Make a recurring daily appointment to spend time with the head mechanic, Jesus. By the way, I don't have time to develop a great closing thought on this topic because I have to rush to the airport to catch a flight to Boston. I know you understand. ☺

chapter thirty-two

'THERE'S NOTHING I CAN DO'

"Whenever anyone says 'I can't,' it
makes me wish he'd get stung to death
by about ten thousand bees. When
he says 'I'll try,' five thousand bees."
—*"Deep Thoughts" by Jack Handey*

I was checking into a hotel in Colorado Springs, Colorado, very late at night because my flight took five hours longer due to a mechanical problem, a weather problem, and a missing co-pilot problem. It took awhile; but the plane was fixed, the weather got better, and they sobered up the co-pilot.

Not a good travel day.

As I walked up to the counter at the hotel, a young lady was keying information into the computer. And without looking up she said, "Name."

So I gave her my two-syllable Tennessean name: *"Tee-um."*

Without changing her monotone voice or looking up, "Last name."

"Steed," I mustered. "It's a horse of course, so you better heed the steed if you want to grow to be a flower, not a weed."

She looked up, then, "Do you have a reservation?"

At this point I was thinking that I had better act right. "Yes," I firmly stated, "non-smoking, overlooking the Atlantic." (I said I was *thinking* about acting right, not actually following through with such an outlandish idea.)

She started keying in more information and frowned, "We have you down for a smoking, two double beds."

I protested, "I had reserved a non-smoking. I'm speaking at a six-hour seminar tomorrow; and a smoking room will not work, thank you."

She gave me the "attitude" look. "Says here you requested a smoking," she stated.

"Did not."

"Did too."

"Did not."

At that she began furiously keying in information.

"Looks like we're full, and all we have left is your smoking room." And with that she slammed down hard on the delete key. I paused, pondering my next move; and then she said something that should never, ever, be said to a customer, client, employee, or vendor under any circumstance: "Anyway, there's nothing I can do."

This is the point where I should have maintained that vow of silence. But I didn't.

"Excuse me? Oh there's something you can do. In fact, there's *plenty* you can do, young lady. First off, you ever think since you're in the hospitality industry, one of your jobs is to be hospitable? So you *could* be hospitable.

"You could do that. You *could* have greeted me with a smile and a pleasant voice when I walked up after traveling all day. You *could* have called me 'Sir,' or 'Mr. Steed,' and said, 'Yes, sir' and 'No, sir.'

"You *could* have used a rarely practiced system of behavior called, 'good manners.' You *could* have done lots of things besides standing behind that counter with one of the worst cases of non-caring attitude I've ever witnessed.

"Now, let's start over, Missy Miss; but this time, think of things you *can* do, not what you *can't* do. Now, take a deep breath and tell me, what *can* you do?"

She stared at me blankly, "I *can* call security."

That one caught me off guard. "Let me rephrase that," I said. "What *can* you do that does not involve me calling my wife for bail money?"

And finally she began thinking not of the barrier, and that's key—not focusing on the barrier but on the "how" of creatively solving my problem and casting her vision of how she could help.

I could see her brain working, "I could call other hotels in the area to see if they have a non-smoking room with a comparable rate."

I encouraged her, "Excellent! What else can you do?"

Her smile got bigger, "I could give you a free continental breakfast."

I was stumped, "Aren't those free anyway?"

Her brain launched back into activity, "I could have Elrod bring it to your room in the morning. I could call the general manager at home and wake her up in the middle of the night and tell her I'm dealing with a difficult situation. I could give you the 1-800 number

to our corporate headquarters so you could complain to them."
Then she stopped, amazed at all her possible solutions.

At this point, I wanted to patch up the relationship and become more personal with her. So I looked at her name tag and said, "Velcrola? I would like to apologize to you for my being such a jerk. I'm very immature in the worst possible moments, and I let my temper get the best of me when I'm tired. I yell at people when I think I'm not getting my way, and then I have the habit of treating them in a condescending and sarcastic manner. I'm also very egotistical and prone to outbreaks of selfish, unrelenting hypocrisy. But there's nothing I can do. I know you understand."

I gave her my best smile and walked away to my smoking room, knowing I would sleep very well that night. ☺

MUST-HEAR SERMON:

**Don't Bite the
Hand That Feeds You
Unless You Haven't
Had Dinner**

chapter thirty-three

LIFE-AFTER-DEATH BOOKS

"Heaven—the treasury
of everlasting life."
—*William Shakespeare*

I was browsing in a bookstore and found a section called,
"Life After Death." And that caught my eye because there were
close to 50 different books on what happens to you when you go
to Heaven. You've probably read some of them yourself or heard
about them; but the life-after-death books are written by regular
(as opposed to irregular) people who were officially pronounced
dead, went to Heaven, and then came back to their bodies, where
they were then officially pronounced alive.

Accordingly, the first thing these people do once they get their
health back is to write a book about their experiences. And that's
fine, but what really gets me is that not one author offers up actual
proof that he or she went to Heaven.

No physical evidence of any kind turns me into a doubting
Thomas because I would like some kind of proof of these bold
claims. I don't need anything major or earth shattering either. I

would just like to see someone at the grocery store wearing an "I went to Heaven, and all I got was this lousy T-shirt," shirt. That would pretty much settle the issue for me.

Think about it, when somebody goes to Heaven and then comes back to Earth, don't you think he'd bring back—at the very least—a souvenir? People bring back souvenirs from Biloxi, Mississippi, of all places; so you know Heaven would be a "Been there, done that!" kind of place to purchase a memento.

If you're going to tell me the story, then have a toothpick holder, bumper sticker, or ashtray to go along with it. I know when I go to Heaven I'm going to be asking about an outlet mall because if God returns me to Earth, the first thing my family members are going to ask is, "What'd you bring us back?"

I'll pull out my suitcase, "I have a box of celestial salt-water taffy and a half-pound of infinity fudge. And I bought everyone their own personalized air-brushed license plate you can put on the front of your car." Then they'll all hug me, and I'll write a best-selling book about it, offering up pictures and store receipts as proof I went to Heaven.

One thing I noticed is that most of the life-after-death books follow a pattern of storytelling about going to Heaven. The first thing is, if you want to return to your body, you have to follow procedure. And procedure states that when you die, you exit your body and hover over it for a short period of time. As you hover, you look at yourself until that gets boring; and then suddenly, without much fanfare, you find yourself in the famous "dark tunnel." Those are steps 1, 2, and 3 for these books: expire, hover, dark tunnel.

As far as I can tell, most of the authors say the same thing about the tunnel, "I found myself speeding through a dark tunnel." Or, "I was racing through a dark tunnel."

I have a problem with that description because everyone always goes fast through the tunnel. I think if the dark tunnel thing were true, at least one author would write, "I arrived at a dark tunnel, and it was backed up due to construction. They had all these orange-and-white barrels forcing it down to one lane. People were actually cutting each other off to get a better spot in line. And there was this real jerk behind me yelling, 'Come on! This is taking an eternity!'"

Now if *that* scenario were in a life-after-death book, I would believe it, no doubt.

Continuing with procedure, the next step after speeding through the tunnel is your encounter with the even-more-famous "loving bright light." Every single life-after-death book pays tribute to the "loving bright light." And the authors all say they wanted nothing more than to go inside the light, and they felt they had to keep moving toward the light.

Wouldn't it be ironic if the loving bright light were God's version of the backyard bug zapper? "There's the light! It's loving! It's forgiving! It's ..." PHHHZZZZT! It's over.

After the loving bright light, the writers say that they found themselves in a personal meeting with God. And some write that they actually received a free tour of Heaven as well. They write that they wanted to ask God all kinds of questions on the tour; but He could read their minds, and they could read His, so no one really talked. I guess they just kind of looked around and marveled.

The last thing that happens to you, the authors say, is that God tells you you've got to go back to Earth. And you ask, "Why?" And He responds, "You're smart. You'll figure it out." And before you can ask for somebody to take you to a store so you can buy a tacky souvenir, you find yourself back in your body and visiting with an editor who's going to clean up the grammar and punctuation of your book.

Think about it, when somebody goes to Heaven and then comes back to Earth, don't you think he'd bring back—at the very least—a souvenir?

And that's pretty much what happens in the life-after-death books. So let's explore just a scant few things the Bible says about Heaven. The actual word *Heaven* appears hundreds of times in the Scriptures. Jesus referenced Heaven many, many times. Read the book of Matthew and you'll see that our Lord compared Heaven to a mustard seed, a man who sowed good seed, a kind of yeast, a treasure hidden in a field, a merchant looking for fine pearls, and a net that catches fish. He also taught us we should, "Repent, for the kingdom of heaven is near."

The Book of Revelation tells us—not literally but figuratively—what Heaven and the new Earth will look like, so you may want to spend some time studying John's vision of everlasting life. But my favorite quote concerning Heaven is what Saint Paul taught in Philippians 3:20: "Our citizenship is in heaven. And we eagerly await a Savior from there, the Lord Jesus Christ."

To me, that verse speaks volumes. No matter how we get there—a dark tunnel, unexpected rapture, or a crowded shuttle bus—Heaven is the true home for followers of Christ. We might not know *exactly* what it looks like and what all happens there, but we can take great joy and comfort that this unseen place called Heaven is our eternal, loving home. ☉

chapter thirty-four

THREE-DAY FAST

"The best of all medicines
is resting and fasting."
—*Benjamin Franklin*

I went on a three-day fast. No food, no coffee, no electronic media; just water. Water for three whole days; and I grew spiritually, and I grew humps on my back. Jesus told us in Matthew 6:16, "When you fast, do not look somber as the hypocrites do, for they disfigure their faces to show men they are fasting." But there's no way to hide humps, especially if you wear a lot of knit shirts. People try to be helpful and invite you to walk around in their kid's sandbox. "Just trying to make you feel at home, Camel Boy," they say.

You might want to know why I fasted for three days. It's simple: three is a Scriptural number. I know, so is 40. I like three better. Now I bet you're thinking that seven is also a Scriptural number. You're right, but I still like three because of its *shortness*.

Actually, the idea of a three-day fast was planted in my head by a fine Christian woman at my church from whom I don't take advice anymore. She shared about how she had gone on a three-day fast to seek God's perfect will and direction for her life. And she told me at the end of the third day how her eyes were opened—by the paramedics. I thought, *I could fast. It might be fun to faint from lack of nutrients.*

My main motivation was that I really wanted to hear and understand God's perfect will and direction for me. So I fasted. I kept a journal as well to capture my thoughts and the Lord's guidance.

Day 1: Hey, not bad.

Day 2: Hump Day, baby! (Sorry.)

Day 3: God hasn't spoken, and I'm having Internet withdrawals.

I was confused after the fast. Why didn't God speak to me? I had Bible study. I had prayer time. I had humps.

Actually I did have one impression, if you will, that came to me right before I sat down to eat at the end of the third day. And the impression was: "Study the Bible."

It was so fleeting of an impression, really, that I almost thought it didn't happen. Three days of no coffee, no sports page, no Internet, no "Larry King Live." But there it was: "Study the Bible."

Come on, God. I need something more than that. I sacrificed a lot. Where's the burning bush? Where's the blinding light? Where's the small person sitting in a tree wearing a Waffle House hat? At the very least, You could have had an angel FedEx Your will to me. Three days of suffering, and You told me something I already knew?

But there's a difference between knowing and doing. I wasn't doing.

And so I went back to my old habits of sporadically "reading" the Bible complemented by a not-so-effective, rushed prayer time. Sadly, I missed both opportunities and blessings for about a year,

---

> One thing that struck me and resonated with me was that I didn't know all of the commandments of Jesus. And to know them, I have to study them.

---

until one day I was sleepily sitting in Sunday School class (or as I like to call it, "Bible study"); and my teacher, Russ Lott, had us break down The Great Commission. (It's in Matthew 28. Go look it up; it'll be good for you.) And folks, I'm here to tell you we broke that sucker down word by word, phrase by phrase. To scrutinize that one, simple verse took 45 minutes of the lesson. *That's* studying the Bible.

And the one thing that struck me and resonated with me was that I didn't know all of the commandments of Jesus. And to know them, I have to study them. I have to hear them spoken by my teacher and pastor. I have to use them. They have to be a part of me.

So, for those of you thinking about fasting for three days, take my advice and start off with a shorter time—like 10 minutes. Then work your way up. God will be glad you did. The world will be glad you did. And your stomach will be really, really happy about it as well. ☺

chapter thirty-five

TIP JARS

"It is inhumane, in my opinion, to force
people who have a genuine medical
need for coffee to wait in line behind
people who apparently view it as
some kind of recreational activity."
—*Dave Barry*

Have you been keeping track of how a growing number
of businesses today want something for nothing? Used to be that
businesses would take your money and give you something in
exchange. But today, businesses take your money and give you
nothing in exchange. Like coffee shops, they're great at getting
something for nothing. From the big chains to the cool, little mom-
and-pop stores, coffee shops are notorious for putting out a tip jar
next to the cash register.

My question is: What extra service do they provide for us to tip
them? Do they put in the cream and sugar for us? No, they give us
the cup and tell us to help ourselves at the creamer kiosk. Do they
greet us at the door and show us to a table? No, we walk in, stand

in line, get our java, and then find a place to sit on our own. Do they smilingly stop by and take the empty cups and napkins and sincerely inquire about our caffeine concerns? No, we just get up and throw all that stuff away when we leave.

And yet the tip jar is ever-present on the counter. What gets me is that there is always money in the tip jar. I see ones and fives and a whole lot of quarters. I think the coffee people are saving up for a down payment on a new house in a gated community.

Now you might laugh, but let's say you purchase a small cup of coffee. They charge you $3.12. You give them $4; and as they give you back your change, they discreetly nod toward the tip jar. So not wanting to be cheap like me, you drop the 88 cents into the jar.

But this doesn't happen just once a day; it happens over 300 times a day. Oh yeah, 300 times a day they rake in 88 cents. Here's what I want you to do: multiply that daily total times 365. If my math skills are in working order, coffee shop employees are taking in over $96,000 in unreported income a year. That's $96,000 for giving someone a latte and nodding toward a tip jar. Not a bad living for not going above and beyond your job description.

Now please don't misread me here. I'm all for helping people. And I'm all for putting money in those plastic jugs at gas stations where someone needs money for surgery. But I'm against putting money in a tip jar that employees set out. I saw a tip jar in the express lane at my grocery store. It had a sign above it: "You scan it, you bag it, you give us your change." And then in small print: "You take it out, you put it in your car, and you like it."

My fear is that this trend will catch on with all types of businesses. Just think, what if your dentist put out a tip jar? "Time for your tooth extraction, and by the way, here's my tip jar." I think you would have no choice but to tip—and to tip *heavily*.

Or what if the person who does your taxes put out a tip jar? What if your mail carrier put out a tip jar? What if the school crossing guard lady put out a tip jar?

CROSSING GUARD LADY: You know, I have a hard time watching all these kids and the cars at the same time. It's kind of confusing...

PETRIFIED PARENT: All I have on me is a couple of quarters.

CROSSING GUARD LADY: That'll get her across this morning. This afternoon, when traffic is heavier, now that might be a different story. But for now, she's OK.

We may soon get to the point where banks will just go ahead and put a barcode right on our foreheads. Businesses will scan us from 100 yards out in the parking lot. That's where our world is heading: "I want everything you have, and I give nothing or very little in return."

I think God even has out a tip jar. But He doesn't just want our spare change; He wants our entire bank account. And He doesn't just want some of us some of the time; He wants every ounce of fiber in our being at all times.

God wants our actions and our thoughts and our money and bodies and our jobs and our families. But the difference between

God and a coffee shop is that God gives us *everything* in return. God gives us His Son, God gives us His Helper, and God gives us life forever.

God doesn't just want some of us some of the time; He wants every ounce of fiber in our being at all times.

The next time you're out and about, stop and be aware that God has set out His tip jar. Then thank Him, and reach in and give Him everything you have. The returns are incredible. ☯

chapter thirty-six

MALL WALKERS

"The legs are the wheels of creativity."
—*Albert Einstein*

Have you ever felt like you were doing the right thing but in the wrong place? Mall walkers would come to mind as an example. They're exercising (right thing) but in the wrong place (crowded mall).

The reason I know it's the wrong place is because I was viciously sideswiped by a reckless mall walker. The unexpected impact by the speeding walker (who was NOT using a hands-free cell phone) threw me right into the entrance of Victoria's Secret, where my wife found me dazed and confused.

And so—amongst the over-priced lingerie—I was now bruised, embarrassed, and humiliated. I ran back out of the store, but that ruthless mall walker just kept on trucking along as if nothing had happened. I was going to yell at him for his total disregard for shopping safety, but I stopped myself when I noticed he was being led by a seeing-eye rottweiler. On occasion, I know when to use the vow of silence to my advantage.

The whole frightening incident, which still has me shaking, started me thinking that I should begin a petition. And I'm positive I could get enough names on the list so that our lawmakers could process legislation that makes it illegal to exercise in areas designed for shopping. I know what you're thinking, "When mall walking is outlawed, only outlaws will mall walk." And that's exactly when we'll arrest them and clean up the riffraff in America.

So, if you are a mall walker, and you're reading this right now, I make this earnest plea: Please exercise in a place that was created for exercising—your local freeway. I know you're doing a good thing by taking care of your health, but the mall is a bad place to work out. To me, it's like taking your family to pick up litter in the community and choosing a crack neighborhood at night in which to do it.

FATHER: OK, we'll just park my brand-new SUV under this broken-out street light. We'll start at that condemned house that looks to be crawling with suspicious gang activity.

SISSY: Great, Dad. And I'm going to wear all the gold jewelry I can possibly fit on my body, 'k?

JUNIOR: And I'll go ahead and paste these $20 bills right to my forehead!

FATHER: Fantastic! Now remember, once we get out, let's all split up. We'll meet back up later at the morgue.

Right thing: picking up litter. Wrong place: crack neighborhood in the middle of the night.

As a Christian, have you ever wondered if you're doing the right thing as a servant of Christ but perhaps in the wrong place?

A good friend of mine, Jen Gash, was knee-deep in church activities. She was a leader at church and was serving in many different and busy ways. But it wasn't until she took a mission trip overseas that she discovered her true ministry, serving the orphans of Moldova.

Take time to assess your heart and your activities as they relate to being productive for the Kingdom.

She came back to the States, quit her job, quit her various and sundry church jobs, and started an organization called Sweet Sleep that helps take care of the unwanted children of Moldova. And now Sweet Sleep has grown to become part of Children's Emergency Relief International, and Jen Gash is happily doing the right thing in the right place.

Take time to assess your heart and your activities as they relate to being productive for the Kingdom. Are you doing the right things? If so, are you doing them in the right places? And if not, where might those right places be?

To help with clarity in your decision-making, get out of your normal environment to walk, think, and pray. Head somewhere you can walk without interruption, and you might just discover where the right place is to do your right thing. Just don't pick a mall to do your walking. ☉

chapter thirty-seven

SIX PRINCIPLES FOR PRODUCTIVE SLEEPING IN CHURCH

"I usually take a two-hour nap from 1-4."
—*Yogi Berra*

As most of us have learned throughout the years, taking a power nap or just downright sleeping in church can be a difficult goal to achieve. However with a little pre-planning, it's possible to get that uninterrupted shut-eye you so rightly deserve. To that end, I've developed six workable principles for productive sleeping during a church service that, if followed religiously, will guarantee you'll be feeling your spiritual best by the time worship is over and you're headed to your car.

Feng Shui the people in your congregation.

The National Sleep Institute of Lower Arkansas reveals that 72 percent of the people who sleep in church, sleep better when others around them are organized in a logical and balanced manner. Feng Shui can help. For those of you who might not be familiar with the concept of Feng Shui, it's the age-old Chinese practice of living in harmony with colors, materials, and homeowners associations.

The idea would be to pay the ushers to coordinate people wearing like-colored clothing, as well as comparable body weights, together in small cluster groups throughout the sanctuary. Now at first, this might seem like an insurmountable task, but most ushers I know will take a small bribe if it's presented to them in unmarked bills. And once you have all the people in church sitting in complete harmonious balance, you're ready to choose your pew location.

Never sit on the back pew.

The back pew is the absolute worst place to sleep during church. One reason is that it's the most crowded row in church, so you don't have much elbow room or shoulder room to get a restful snooze. And add in the fact that people are always leaving the service early from the back row, and you'll soon come to the conclusion that it's virtually impossible to siesta while the people exiting are "accidentally" stepping on your toes. A better choice of seat would be in the middle section of the pews. In fact, reserve your prime location in advance by putting your Bible/prop in the spot in which you wish to sit.

If you're not entirely happy with your choice of seat, then scan the sanctuary for a better pew during the pre-sermon prayer. When you spy that more preferred seat, quietly get up and move while people have their heads bowed and eyes closed. I do this all the time, and it works relatively well. However, my wife and daughter have a big problem with embarrassing themselves, so they always stubbornly remain in their seats.

Make sure your body and mind are tired.

It's really important to be physically and mentally exhausted before sleeping in church. Abstain from coffee and doughnuts in Sunday School, or skip Sunday School altogether. Instead, take a brisk walk around the church parking lot while multiplying fractions in your head. By the time you reach your seat, you'll be totally worn out and ready to snore up a storm.

One more item that's often overlooked is eating a heavy pre-sermon meal. It's been documented and proven repeatedly by the Scientific Antarctic Meat-Lovers Research Committee that you rest much better on a full stomach, and you could even reach a wonderful state of sleep called "Blissful Hibernation." My favorite pre-sermon meal is pasta, pork chops, and cheesecake. Just be careful and watch the amount you eat, as you don't want to enter into an unexpected eternal blissful hibernation, if you get my drift.

Tell people around you of your intentions.

Before actually nodding off, be sure to alert your neighbors of your plans to sleep. They'll make a point not to bother you, and they'll pass the collection plate right past you. Also, they'll be more forgiving of you when you put your feet up in the pew and lay your head on their shoulder. But please no drooling, people find that offensive.

Conversely, don't inform any kids within spitball distance that you're going to catch 40 winks. They'll do their best to keep you awake with a slimy bombardment made from the church bulletin just for the plain joy of it. It's true, not everyone needs to know of your plans. I actually know of one church member who stood up right before the sermon, held up his arms like Moses parting the Red Sea, and issued a nap decree to the entire congregation. Big mistake as the preacher also heard him and made him walk up to the platform and give his 15-minute testimony. Folks, there's a big difference between *sleeping* in public and *speaking* in public, so please be careful.

Wear comfortable clothes.

Right off the bat, I have to say: wear your slippers. That's right, comfortable slippers are a must for a good Sunday morning, REM-type doze. However, if you don't feel at ease wearing your slippers into church, then put them in a brown paper bag and carry them in. Your feet should be relaxed and not crunched into a pair of tight-fitting high heels, especially if you happen to be a respected deacon.

As far as clothes, wear something loose fitting like a tank top and sweat pants. Never wear a tie or a scarf or even a hat. Those are constricting and offer very little comfort. If your church is always cold, pack an L.L. Bean goose-down jacket or make friends with someone at church who always dresses in layers. If that person knows you're napping, being of Christian heart, he or she will give you something to keep you warm.

Bring your stuff.

Think day at the beach. Bring anything and everything that will help you drift off quickly. Try a wrap-around travel pillow, decorative eye mask, earplugs, a small airline blanket, and bottled water. You may not need them all, but it's better to have them on hand

---

Take a brisk walk around the church parking lot while multiplying fractions in your head. By the time you reach your seat, you'll be totally worn out and ready to snore up a storm.

---

as a precaution. There's nothing worse than nodding off as the preacher starts waxing poetic and then realizing you could use a cool sip of water to help you find slumber-land.

Also consider bringing in other resources that will help you sleep, like one of the 7 Habits books by Steven Covey or any Mary Kate and Ashley DVD. If you happen to know someone good at doing impressions, see if he'll sit by you and make the sounds of gentle waves breaking on a shoreline. And as always, consult your physician before using any type of sleeping pill, sleeping patch, or sleeping injection.

So there you have it: six principles for productive sleeping in church. Remember, catching some much-needed z's on Sunday morning is an art; and if you follow just a few simple guidelines, you'll always leave church feeling refreshed and ready to face the world on Monday morning.

Happy napping! ☺

chapter thirty-eight

THE CHURCH PARKING NAZI

"...the fruit of the Spirit is
love, joy, peace, patience, kind-
ness, goodness, faithfulness,
gentleness and self-control..."
—*Galatians 5:22-23*

I'm a volunteer parking lot attendant at my megachurch,
Brentwood Baptist, in Brentwood, Tennessee. Our pastor, Mike
Glenn, refers to us as "ministers." However, most of the congregation refers to us as "targets." To the people driving too fast,
sipping hot coffee, and talking on their cell phones while driving
one-handed, we're physical targets. To those who don't like policy
and procedure, we're verbal targets. And to those who flunked out
of their court-ordered anger management classes, we're both.

One beautiful Sunday morning, a well-dressed man called us
"Nazis" because I had the audacity to help guide him into a pre-
selected parking space. He jumped out of his car, veins popping
on his neck and forehead, nostrils flaring, and pointing a long,

splintery (index) finger at me, he screamed, "You're a Nazi! In fact, all you parking people are Nazis!"

The first thing that came to my mind was not thinking that statement should be offensive; but instead, I was quickly reminded of an episode from "Seinfeld" called "The Soup Nazi." So I said, "You! Leave! No parking spot for you. Come back—one year."

For future reference, when in a conflict situation, don't quote jokes from a sitcom if the other person has no sense of humor. It tends to escalate things to the point where law enforcement intervention is necessary. However, my jail time was short, and I was reminded—once again—that keeping your mouth closed by taking a vow of silence in stressful situations is actually beneficial to you in the long run.

On a different Sunday morning, one of the members of the parking lot Gestapo, er...team, Otis Reichsfuhrer, reported to me that a lady verbally accosted him after exiting her vehicle: "You have no clue what you're doing. None at all! This parking lot is the most totally messed up thing I've ever seen. Do they let crazy people park us? Is that it?"

Now, I must admit that Otis shouldn't have tried to guide her sub-compact beneath a Hummer. But it was Easter Sunday, and we were under strict orders by the SS (Sunday School) to double park as many small cars as possible. Otis just thought that parking one vehicle under another one qualified as double parking.

Another dedicated parking attendant from the Special Events Panzer Division, Jason Himmelshutzen, said a man approached him after experiencing a Baptist blitzkrieg. A Baptist blitzkrieg is when we open the floodgates and bring everyone roaring in at once. It's kind of like they do at Disney World, so our goal is to park as many sleep-deprived Southern Baptists in a row as fast as we possibly can.

"You bring us in too fast, and we're not even awake yet. And then you park us too tight next to each other so I have to sit there and wait for the little kids or the elderly to get out of their cars before I can get out of my own car. It's ridiculous! It's all I can do not to curse you guys before going in to worship."

Actually, we hear that last sentence rather frequently; and we should because our Parking Lot Ministry mission statement reads, in part, "To park cars efficiently and quickly while giving Christians the opportunity to use profanity."

But no matter the aggravations we go through and the bad attitudes we experience, the thing that makes me smile is knowing that a high percentage of people who get upset, angry, and psycho with us before going into church will come out in a much different spirit after church. It seems like in just a matter of an hour or two, the parking lot attendants go from being seen as brutal, heartless Nazis to the blessed Allied Forces of the living God.

The person who chewed us up and spit us out for showing him where to park will come back out and, in a display of heartfelt meekness, thank us for doing a great job. He'll make a point to now pat us on the back, whereas before he wanted to stab us in the back. These once-livid patrons will drive past us and not swerve the vehicle at us like before; but instead, they'll roll down their windows and present us with cookies, drinks, and cash prizes.

One lady threatened a nasty, drawn-out lawsuit because she said we profiled her as a Georgia Bulldogs fan. She accused us of—acting with much forethought and malicious premeditation—giving her the absolute worst spot in the entire 14-acre lot due to her allegiance to that particular football team.

Let's all get up a little earlier and serve God with worship before we come to God's worship service.

Then after the church service, the lawsuit lady showed up and presented one of our grizzled veterans, Colonel Chris Klink, with a small, single daisy. Now, there was an angry yellow jacket in the flower; and it repeatedly stung Colonel Klink about the face and neck. But it really was a touching moment, and we'll always remember her humility rather than his allergic reaction and subsequent ambulance ride.

By the way, just so I can clear the air, the lawsuit lady was correct about our collegiate profiling. We do look for cars that blatantly display rival team colors. If you have license plates, bumper stickers, or flag colors besides the orange and white of the University of Tennessee, we'll park you in Mongolia. Those who have ears, let them hear.

Indeed, the transformation we witness from our perspective as attendants is truly amazing. But it would be a much nicer parking lot, and world for that matter, if those who are just like me—people prone to impatience, anger, and ego—would make a commitment to change our hearts before we arrived at church. Let's all get up a little earlier and serve God with worship before we come to God's worship service. And then let's show up not only at the church parking lot but at our sometimes stressful jobs, at the long lines at the grocery stores, and at the numerous traffic jams with the fruit of the Spirit already ripe and ready to be shared with others.

In other words, let's have church before coming to church. And if that happens at churches all across America, then I'll stop the unfair profiling of college football fans. You have my word as a National Socialist church parking attendant. ☉

TIM STEED

For almost a quarter of a century, Tim Steed has impacted the lives of over a million people with his keynote speeches, corporate seminars, comedy routines, television shows, video productions, college orientation programs, high school programs, actor seminars, and professional theater.

Tim began his performance career at Roane State Community College in Knoxville, Tennessee. It was there that a speech teacher asked him to try out for a play. While still in school, he began acting in professional outdoor dramas such as *The Smoky Mountain Passion Play*.

Then, at the University of Tennessee, Tim discovered stand-up comedy and took home the First Runner-up prize for the "Funniest Person on Campus." He continued to hone his comedy routines at places like the Comedy Zone and The Funny Bone while still in school. During this time he also met a group of local actors in an improvisational theatre company called "On the Edge." Tim helped take the group from performing on the stage at the historic Bijou Theater in Knoxville to writing and producing their own television shows.

Inspired by his local success, Tim moved to Orlando, Florida, to find new opportunities in television. "My big break came when

I was killed by the 'Swamp Thing' on the USA Network. Casting agents liked the way I gurgled when he snapped my neck."

From there he was invited to help launch a new television station, UPN 65. "It was so exciting the day we went on the air. I gave the test pattern a standing ovation."

Enjoying his leadership position, Tim did everything at UPN 65 from writing copy to producing to hosting shows; and his career was picking up steam.

"But I really missed the immediate, face-to-face impact of empowering people while entertaining them at the same time," he recalls. So Tim moved to Nashville, Tennessee, to start his company, Steed Communications, LLC.

He is now recognized as one of the most entertaining and compelling speakers in America. The reason? Tim combines his business leadership background with his entertainment background to produce memorable, content-driven programs that are jam-packed full of relatable humor.

As a Christian inspirational humorist, his presentations offer not just stand-up comedy but spiritual guidance and encouragement for people of all ages. His mission is to empower Christians to fulfill their potential and equip them with the necessary tools to do so while making them laugh.

To book Tim for a speaking engagement, call (615) 833-2052 or visit his Web site, *www.TimSteed.com*.

Tim now lives in Brentwood, Tennessee, with his wife and daughter and their loyal dog, Biscuit. ☺